A LOVER'S QUARREL
WITH THE WORLD

A LOVER'S QUARREL WITH THE WORLD

R. MAURICE BOYD

Edited by Ian A. Hunter

Foreword by Malcolm Muggeridge

The Westminster Press
Philadelphia

Unless otherwise indicated, scripture quotations are from *The New English Bible*. © The Delegates of the Oxford University Press and The Syndics of the Cambridge University Press, 1961, 1970. Used by permission.

First American edition

Published by The Westminster Press®
Philadelphia, Pennsylvania

PRINTED IN THE UNITED STATES OF AMERICA

9 8 7 6 5 4 3 2 1

Library of Congress Cataloging-in-Publication Data

Boyd, R. Maurice, 1932–
    A lover's quarrel with the world.

    1. United Church of Canada—Sermons. 2. United churches—Sermons. 3. Sermons, English—Canada. I. Hunter, Ian, 1945–   II. Title.
BX9882.B69   1988   252'.0792   88-10764
ISBN 0-664-25045-9 (pbk.)

CONTENTS

FOREWORD

There was a time, not so very long ago, when volumes of sermons were in considerable demand. Nowadays, such ponderous works would find few readers and no publishers. The very word "sermon" has come to have a forbidding flavour; in the Oxford English Dictionary a variety of definitions are given, the most suitable of which to convey Maurice Boyd's offerings would seem to me to be: "A discourse (spoken or written) on a serious subject, and containing instruction or exhortation."

Maurice Boyd's offerings are lively, topical, and stimulating. He deals with profound matters lightly and with light matters seriously, managing—a rare quality among preachers today—not to pontificate; rather, to explore the ironies, contradictions, and confusion of our troubled times. In old age I have come to see that in our mortal existence nothing is more beautiful and wonderful than an honest mind searching for truth in the context of a loving soul and a humble and a contrite heart. A good example is Blaise Pascal in the seventeenth century, a great scholar, inventor, and scientist, who put aside his knowledge to cultivate his faith. Or William Blake a century later, who scrawled across the title page of Francis Bacon's *Advancement of Learning* "Good advice for Satan's Kingdom," thereby denouncing the Enlightenment before it had happened. Or in our own time, Mother Teresa dedicating her life to the proposition of love in a world largely given over to the fantasies of power.

It is this quality of an honest mind questing for truth, I should suppose, that Sunday after Sunday attracts large congregations to wherever Maurice Boyd holds forth. I first made his acquaintance at Metropolitan United Church in London, Ontario, some years ago when Professor Ian Hunter and I swapped houses; he to enjoy a sabbatical in Sussex, I as an old practitioner from Fleet Street to do a stint at the University of Western Ontario School of Journalism.

Maurice Boyd proved to be a most engaging neighbour, and did me the honour of inviting me to address his bumper congregation at a Sunday morning service. Then I had the pleasure of meeting him again when he was a stand-in at one of those City churches in London, England, which once were crowded on Sundays with eager worshippers and now tend to have empty pews, their former occupants preferring the everlasting motorways. As P. G. Wodehouse put it: "On Sunday mornings everyone in Little Neck drives to Great Neck, and everyone in Great Neck to Little Neck." Our meeting in the City was blessed by having tea with Mother Teresa.

If I were to offer a criticism of Maurice Boyd's sermons it would be that he is inclined to take Science too seriously. For instance, Darwinian evolution, which, I am quite sure, will amuse posterity for generations to come by the enormous assumptions drawn from such trifling and dubious evidence; seeing, for instance, a direct line of development from primaeval slime to, say, Bertrand Russell.

Near where I live in Sussex there is a public house with the sign "Piltdown Man," to whom when I happen to pass by I always give a respectful salute. The Piltdown Man was originally discovered in the shape of some assorted bones on an anthropological site and became the subject of some five hundred doctoral theses. Teilhard de Chardin was among the students who took him seriously. Then it turned out that the bones had been gathered together by a practical joker who did not even bother to ensure that they came from the same carcass, but just buried them on the site in a shallow grave. Truly God is not mocked!

As I was going over all this in my mind it occurred to me that if I happened to be once more in London, Ontario, and if Maurice Boyd were to ask me again to address his congregation, I should choose as my theme: "Life is a drama, not a process."

MALCOLM MUGGERIDGE

Sussex, 1985

INTRODUCTION

I first heard *of* Maurice Boyd long before I actually heard him preach. Almost from his arrival, friends and acquaintances told me of an extraordinary preacher who combined intellectual integrity with depth, compassion with charisma, so much so that Metropolitan United Church in London, Ontario, had instituted a second morning service to accommodate the overflow congregation. Even though Maurice Boyd was a near neighbour, still I stayed away; my attitude, I suppose, could be summed up as: Can any good thing come of the United Church of Canada? Only in 1983, when my own Anglican Rector went on a brief sabbatical, did I begin to attend Metropolitan to hear Maurice Boyd preach. By this time Metropolitan had become the largest congregation of the United Church of Canada.

Almost as appealing as his preaching, when finally I discovered it, was Maurice Boyd's humour and delight in walking. Thenceforth we passed many pleasurable hours tramping through the neighbourhood talking and laughing volubly—humour bearing much the same relation to faith as harmony to music. The portentous and the power-seeker (often one and the same) seldom laugh; the true Christian must surely chuckle if ever the pearly gates swing open for him. And should there not be an answering peal of celestial laughter, he may well consider that he is at the other place. St. Paul compared the word of God to a two-edged sword; Maurice Boyd wields it adroitly, often to puncture humbug or sanctimoniousness. One of his favourite axioms is that at the heart of Christianity is the message: "Oh, come off it!" On one such stroll, on a warm spring afternoon, I suggested that Maurice publish the sermon he had preached that morning (*Secret Disciples*). My suggestion was hardly novel. His congregations had been making similar requests for years. Maurice explained that his reluctance arose from the fact that he had two new sermons to prepare each week (in addition to weddings, funerals, visitations, and the countless other demands on a minister's time) and that he must occupy his mind with next week's topic, not with polishing last week's. He asked, however, if I would select and edit such a collection. Later we passed several enjoyable days at his tranquil cottage, "Innisfree," overlooking the blue-green waters of Georgian Bay, and we discussed the project, in particular how such a selection might be made. This book is the result.

One or two editorial explanations are in order. Each sermon was revised, in some cases rewritten, for publication. Speaking and writing are as different from each other as the voice is from the pen. I have exercised a free hand as editor to expand, contract, or change, so long as the original meaning is preserved in the transition. Nonetheless, I have also tried to preserve a vestige of the informal sermon style, and I would be delighted if the preacher's voice, even the Irish brogue, occasionally breaks in upon the reader.

In deciding what sermons to include (a difficult task, given Maurice's originality and trenchancy) I have kept in mind three broad categories: (a) pastoral or counselling: (b) exegetic; and (c) an indefinable category of sermons which somehow seem to capture the distinctiveness of Maurice Boyd's ministry. Beyond saying that *Prevenient Grace* is one such, I leave each reader to sort out which sermon falls within each classification.

The first question any solvent publisher asks is: What is the market? How tempting it would be to answer in generalities—even throwing in a biblical allusion about casting one's bread upon the waters. But we would be dishonest not to admit a hope that the book might reach and benefit three distinct groups of readers. First, past and present members of Maurice Boyd's congregations who first heard these thoughts expressed from the pulpit and who might welcome their preservation in more permanent form. Second, clergymen of all denominations, men and women who each week face the daunting challenge of preparing sermons to counsel, uplift, and rightly divide the word of truth. Given the lamentable level to which much preaching has fallen, it may not be misplaced to hope that such a collection might prove instructive for inexperienced or aspiring preachers. Finally, to struggling Christians, wayfarers all who journey from the City of Destruction to the

Celestial City, tempted, distracted, misled, and confused as we are, all likewise wishing that the way were more easeful or that "they might be troubled no more with either hills or mountains to go over" but who have discovered, as Bunyan's hero Pilgrim and all who come after him discover, that "the way is the way, and there is an end."

We would be remiss not to acknowledge a debt of gratitude to two people.

Milly Chidley's alchemy transformed audio tapes, so kindly provided by Mac and Ruth Brown, to typescript and typescript to manuscript. Though she bore the brunt of the labour, she never complained nor did her enthusiasm flag.

Our joint debt to Malcolm Muggeridge, whose graceful Foreword is only the most recent of his many acts of generosity to both author and editor, cannot be expressed without risk of mawkishness. If there were a Dedication it would be to him. Instead, author and editor record here what so often we have said to each other about Muggeridge: words Maxim Gorky wrote about his friend Leo Tolstoy, when once he came upon Tolstoy at the coast sitting on a rock and looking out to sea:

> In the musing, motionlessness of the old man I felt something fateful, magical, something which went down into the darkness beneath him and stretched up like a searchlight into the blue emptiness above the earth . . . in my soul there was joy and fear, and then everything blended in one happy thought: "I am not an orphan on the earth so long as this man lives on it."

IAN A. HUNTER

London, Ontario

A LOVER'S QUARREL WITH THE WORLD

"All existing things are dear to Thee, and Thou hatest nothing that Thou hast created — why else wouldst Thou have made it? Thou sparest all things because they are Thine, our Lord and Master who lovest all that lives; for Thy imperishable breath is in them all."

The Wisdom of Solomon 11:24; 12:1

The American poet, Robert Frost, one day found himself idly wandering through a cemetery, looking at tombstones. As he strolled he read the inscriptions and the dates and the engraved words encapsulating a human life. Born when, died where, and a few words to sum up a lifetime; words chosen by others to remember a friend or loved one. Frost asked himself what epitaph he would choose for his own tombstone. It's a good question. By what words would you wish to be remembered? Frost decided he wanted these words on his tombstone, "I had a lover's quarrel with the world." And they are. Engraved on Frost's tombstone are those words, "I had a lover's quarrel with the world." If you remember nothing more, you will remember those hauntingly beautiful words; once they lodge in your mind they will not quickly leave you.

I have a lover's quarrel with the world. All the words in this statement are important, but the most important is love. It is a *lover's* quarrel. Love stops a quarrel with the world from becoming too harsh or cynical or despairing. Love speaks of appreciation and compassion and commitment. And yet it is also a quarrel. A quarrel because of our dissatisfaction, our restlessness with things as they are and our sense of what things might be. At Robert Kennedy's funeral, Senator Edward Kennedy quoted his brother's favourite lines, "Some men see things as they are and ask why; I dream things that never were and ask: 'Why not?'" The lover and the quarrel!

A lover's quarrel is like a storm at sea; all the fury is on the surface but underneath there is a deep constant current of love. Honesty forces us to admit that even lovers' quarrels can be upsetting, but the love in them runs deep, and is never in question. And they may also be great fun. I think lovers sometimes choose to argue because it is so much fun making up afterwards.

The difference between a quarrel and a lover's quarrel is well illustrated by two Old Testament prophets, Hosea and Amos. Both had a dispute with Israel and both preached against that nation's faithlessness to God. But while Amos was from Judah in the South, Hosea was from Israel and his quarrel was with his own people. His was a lover's quarrel. Consequently you will notice a tenderness about Hosea which contrasts with the harshness of Amos. Hosea has been called the most Christian of the prophets. The difference between them is simply this, Amos had a quarrel while Hosea had a lover's quarrel. And the lover's quarrel was more creative because there was not only indignation but affection in it.

My message is simply this; make sure that all your quarrels are lover's quarrels. This is the key to a creative and fulfilled life. How do you have a lover's quarrel? Let me suggest five instances.

First, make sure that your quarrels with other people are lover's quarrels.

Have you ever noticed how our disagreements with ourselves are always lover's quarrels? When we do things that disappoint us and say foolish and unkind things that hurt other people, we get angry at ourselves but we never quite give up on ourselves. We somehow manage to separate what we have done from what we are. When we do something foolish, we don't say, "I'm a fool"; we say, "I did a foolish thing." We make excuses for ourselves; "I wasn't myself when I did that." We always manage to keep a little distance between ourselves and our own foolishness. We separate them. We make excuses for ourselves even though we do foolish things. This is natural. It is how we manage to retain our self-respect, our dignity and an appropriate self-love. The quarrels we have with ourselves are lover's quarrels.

But often our quarrels with other people are not like that. We don't separate them from the foolish things that they say or do. We identify them with their foolishness. About ourselves, we say, "I did a foolish thing." When other people do foolish things, we say they are fools. With ourselves, we hate the sin, but manage to love the sinner; with other people, we hate the sin and the sinner. And so we write them off. For us, there is always hope. But other people are hopeless.

Now I can give you an irrefutable instance of this. Driving! You know what we do when driving. We signal left and turn right. Or we turn without making any signal at all. Or we go through a red light. Or we get into the wrong stream of traffic and hold everybody up until some kind heart lets us back into the right lane. When these things happen we say that they are the unusual mistakes of an otherwise excellent driver. Isn't that what you say? But let anybody else go through a red light, or make a wrong turn, or hold us up, and we say that a driver like that ought not to be allowed on the road! We have lover's quarrels with ourselves, but not with other people.

All that Jesus really exhorted us to do was to show other people the same kindness and courtesy that we show ourselves. To love our neighbour as ourselves. If you are going to quarrel with others, let it be a lover's quarrel.

Here is another instance. Make sure that your quarrel with the church is a lover's quarrel.

Some years ago the British journalist, Monica Furlong, wrote a fine little book called *With Love To The Church*. In spite of the title, she blasted the church. She was harsh with many of the church's beliefs and practices; she called the church to task for insensitivity, for being afraid of the senses, for being slow to celebrate, for being narrow, unkind and unworthy. She had a quarrel with the church. But, you see, it was a lover's quarrel. Her book is called "*With love* to the Church." And she goes on to say that, in spite of all her criticism, she belongs to the church and loves the church because she constantly meets people in it who teach her the love of God and who live with few defences. Monica Furlong has a lover's quarrel and it is good that the church should listen to her and be rebuked and healed by her. But I know people who have a quarrel with the church which is not a lover's quarrel. They come with unrealistic expectations. They expect everybody in the church to be a saint. Not many of us are saints. And so the first time they meet a hypocrite in church, they are outraged. They say the church is a disappointment. It is full of hypocrites. They decide not to have anything more to do with it. They forget for a moment that they too are hypocrites. Because their quarrel is not a lover's quarrel, they become petulant. Instead of staying in the church and improving it, they become censorious and supercilious, and leave it to the people who have been such a disappointment to them.

There is much to quarrel with in the church. No one knows that better than I who have spent a lifetime in the church's ministry. I, too, have a quarrel with the church, but it is a lover's quarrel. I remember that in spite of all the things that are less than perfect, there is in the church a sense of the divine presence. Where else do we go to learn of Christ? Where else may we grow in knowledge and love of Him? Where else do we learn what forgiveness is? In every church, in every tradition, in each generation, the church has produced marvellous people, so unlike each other, yet each bearing the likeness of Christ in their self-effacement, in their commitment to truth, and their unquenchable love for the world. Thank God for those people who, in spite of all the imperfections of the church, encounter Christ there, and are made Christ-like by Him. So when the church's imperfections weigh on you, remember such people and forgive the church as we ourselves are forgiven. It was Flannery O'Connor who reminded someone who was thinking of joining the church that sometimes one must suffer as much *from* the church as *for* it. We both cherish it and struggle to endure it. So remember that if the church was as perfect as you expect it to be, there wouldn't be any place for you in it! A perfect church wouldn't let you in.

A third instance. If you have a quarrel with the Christian faith, make sure it is a lover's quarrel.

It used to be that if you wanted to argue with the faith you had to leave the church to do it. People have told me that when they were young and assailed with doubts, their parents or their minister gave them the worst possible advice. Young people who expressed doubts or hesitations about Christian doctrine were told that their doubts were wicked and sinful. Sometimes young people are still given the same treatment. They must just believe, believe what they are told on the authority of the one who tells them! Can you imagine that? And so the doubter ignores his reason or stifles his doubts or puts them into a remote cranny of his mind or, most likely, leaves the church in disgust. There is an old children's chorus called "Sunshine Mountain" which exhorts us to "Turn, turn your back on doubting!" The honest doubter is more likely to turn, turn his back on the church and the faith. If only someone had said to such people, "Look, doubt is the cutting edge of faith. It's a good thing to ask questions." If only somebody had told them that the opposite of faith is not doubt; the opposite of faith is fear. If only they had been told to have a lover's quarrel with the faith many young people who today are outside the church might still be inside.

The story of my life is a lover's quarrel with Christian belief. I love the faith. I shall always be grateful that the church presented me with a coherent doctrine, a formulated body of belief. The Christian faith and the church gave me a sense of what it *means* to believe. That is why I have no patience with ministers or theologians who cavalierly dismiss the established doctrine; the theologian who pops up on the cover of *Time* magazine to announce that God is dead. It is the height of presumption to imagine that St. Paul or St. Augustine or Luther or Thomas Aquinas were old fools who never thought of that. So I wanted to affirm the creed, the church, and the faith. But I tell you that I have had a lover's quarrel with all three all my life. There is hardly a doubt about Christian belief that I haven't had. There is scarcely a question about it that I haven't asked. I have been vexed by every spiritual conundrum. And I have grown, not by credulity, but by skepticism. It is a naive, fatuous, twentieth-century notion that Christians are gullible. The greatest Christians have been the greatest skeptics. I think of St. Augustine and Pascal and Kierkegaard and Swift. In our time I think of C.S. Lewis and Malcolm Muggeridge. Skeptics all, but Christians too. G. K. Chesterton once said a marvellous thing. He said that when people cease to believe in God, it is commonly supposed that they become skeptics and believe in nothing; but the truth is much worse. They believe in

anything. The most credulous people are not believers but unbelievers. I once heard an articulate Christian say, "I am not
credulous enough to be an atheist!"

I should be of little use to you as a minister if I had not been
perplexed by the same doubts, haunted by the same questions, as
you are. Often I have discovered that through doubt, orthodoxy is
strengthened. Doubt is not the enemy of faith but an element in
faith. I have found that doubt has illumined and enriched my faith.
So that I have a faith which isn't just somebody else's; it is not just
the church's faith, it is my own faith. I can say with Dostoevsky,
"My hosanna has come forth from the crucible of my doubts." So
have your doubts, and continue your search, and do not feel guilty
about it. Don't think you must take your doubts and uncertainties
outside the church, bring them along with you when you come!

A great poet said:

> Be patient toward all that is unsolved in your heart, and try to
> love the questions themselves.

In other words, have a lover's quarrel with your faith.

Now, listen! I will say something you may think irreverent.
Have a lover's quarrel with God!

I wish more people would have a lover's quarrel with God.
Does that surprise you?

We need to remember that one of the first charges brought
against the early Christians was that they were atheists. Do you
know why? It was because they quarrelled with all the traditional
views of God, whether Greek or Roman or Hebrew. Once they
believed in the God and Father of our Lord Jesus Christ, they
couldn't believe in any other God. Any other conception of God
was judged by the gracious presence who had made Himself known
in Jesus Christ. They were now Christians, and the God in whom
they believed was the God whom they had encountered in Jesus
Christ.

I meet all kinds of Christians who ought to have a lover's quarrel with their God because the God they believe in is not the God
and Father of our Lord Jesus Christ. He is a monster. All through
my ministry I have met men and women who have believed in a

God so narrow and vindictive and cruel that I wouldn't believe in Him for a minute. And yet they come to the House of God to worship Him. To worship means to ascribe worth. How can one ascribe worth to a God who is not only less than divine, but sometimes less than human?

William Barclay, a fine New Testament scholar and teacher, lost his daughter and son-in-law in a boating accident. They were sailing off the coast of County Antrim, Northern Ireland. A sudden storm came up and both were drowned. After the funeral, William Barclay received an anonymous letter from a woman who called herself a Christian. The letter said, "I know why God killed your daughter and son-in-law; it was because of your heretical teachings." Of course, Barclay couldn't answer this woman because she didn't sign her name. But he said that if he could have answered her he would have done so in the words of John Wesley. He would have said, "My dear lady, if that is the kind of God you believe in, then your God is my devil." That lady needed to have a lover's quarrel with her God. Maybe her ideas about Him would be less distorted and more in harmony with the love and grace which Jesus Christ made incarnate.

A lover's quarrel with God goes on in the Bible itself. That is what Job had. Job said, "In the name of justice I cry out against God who has treated me unjustly!" Job persevered and, in the end, he discovers that all through the great contest he has had with God, God has been on his side. Notice that in the scriptures those who truly believe are sometimes much less reverent than the pious, thoughtless believers. Always in the name of God they are confronting God, demanding an explanation, making a complaint, bringing a charge against Him. And in the end they are usually vindicated and have shown us more of God than we had known before. C. S. Lewis puts it well. He says that when you stand for what you know to be right and good, even against God, in the end you will receive Divine approval. So, have a lover's quarrel with God. Some of us desperately need to.

A few years ago one couple left my congregation to join another church. They did so because they were offended when I said, one Sunday morning, that I did not really believe that God was pleased when Joshua massacred all the people of Jericho. He massacred all the men, women, children, and even the animals. The people who left my church thought that God was pleased by this slaughter. They thought that God ordered an atrocity that would have earned the outrage and condemnation of the United Nations. I hope that couple is happy in the congregation where they now worship. God help them if they still worship that kind of God! Would you want to?

If that is the kind of God you believe in, why worship at all? Stay home and watch television or do crossword puzzles. To worship such a God will not strengthen your character, it will destroy it. If you come to His house to ascribe worth to God, let the God whom you praise be the God who has come close to us in Jesus Christ.

I have said that we should have a lover's quarrel with others, with the Church, with the faith, and with God. One thing more, and it brings me back to Robert Frost's epitaph with which I started. We ought to have a lover's quarrel with the world.

John Gunther was a young man who discovered he had a fatal illness, and he died very young. But he kept a diary. And in his diary he wrote these two luminous sentences, "Contentment with the universe. Discontent with the world."

Contentment with the universe! This is God's creation which He loved into existence. Discontent with the world! That's the quarrel. There is so much in this world that is so difficult to understand. So perplexing. So hard.

Once again, this is the story of my life. I have had a lover's quarrel with the world. When I stand in the pulpit and look out over my congregation, I see in every part of the church people who have been hurt by life, people who have been afflicted with great suffering, who have borne great anxiety. I know many who have experienced great sorrow. All of these things sometimes crowd in on me, and I ask the question, "Why?" Why is the world like this? Why is there cancer? Why do babies become ill? Why are there such terrible accidents? Why is there so much loneliness and hurt and cruelty and injustice? Why is there war?

It would be very difficult to live in our world with all its fierce enigmas and not to have a quarrel with it. And yet, while it is true that I have a quarrel with the world, it is a lover's quarrel. I love the world. I love its beauty, which is a harbinger of another world beyond time. I love its people who reflect the image of their creator. I love the kindness and the love one experiences. I love life. So that before I begin to quarrel, I make an act of affirmation:

Life is sweet brother. Sweet Brother?
There's night and day brother,
Both sweet things;
Sun and moon and stars, brother,
All sweet things.
There's likewise the wind on the heath.
Life is very sweet brother,
Who would wish to die?

This essential goodness of life is something we affirm every time we bring a little child into the world. When we do so, we believe we are doing a good thing, a creative thing. The truth is that we are. We celebrate birthdays and by so doing we affirm that life is good. It was a good day when you were born. Even though the risks to life and limb are great; even though we are threatened from every side by pain, illness, sorrow and death, we nevertheless believe that life is a good gift to bestow. When people commit suicide, having found life insupportable, we do not conclude that life is bad, but rather lament those privations that have obscured its goodness.

Father D'Arcy wrote a book about evil and suffering. He begins by putting them in perspective. Before you start to complain, he writes, just remember that you have life and that life is good. So before we quarrel with the world let us offer an act of thanksgiving to Almighty God who called us into life and being.

You might go just one step further with me on this track. It's a difficult point, but worth grasping. True, we have a lover's quarrel with the world because of all the evil that is in it; but all the evil in the world means but one question in the end. The question is, "Why is the world what it is and not something else?" As accountants say, that is the bottom line. Whatever the affliction or sorrow or suffering or hurt or loneliness, the question raised is, why did God make the world the way it is and not something different?

If you meditate on that question, you will begin to feel the strangeness of it. I suppose God could have made the world

different; but if He had, I might not be around to ask the question.
Do you see my point? Here am I, asking this question about this
world, when it is the only world I know; when it is this world which
has given me life and breath and being. It is from this round earth's
imagined corners that I was called to life. How strange, then, that
when this world has made me all that I am and you what you are,
and given us all that we have, we should complain that it is the way
it is and not something different. If it had been something different,
we might not be around to complain about it. We lament that the
world is not perfect, forgetting that if it were, there might be no
place for us in it, for we fall far short of perfection! So if we are to
quarrel with the world, let us not forget first to love it. Because life is
good. It is a gift of grace. It is God's gift.

One thing more. Robert Frost's tombstone says he had a lover's
quarrel with the world. For a long time I wondered why I loved that
epitaph so much. Then, one day, in a flash, it came to me. I love it
because that is the kind of quarrel God has with the world. Oh, yes,
He has a quarrel! How could He help it? Don't you want Him to
quarrel with some of the things that go on in your life? Would you
expect Him to be satisfied with a world which sometimes disap-
points even you? A world so different from what He longs for it to
be? God has a quarrel with the world. Some say it is a quarrel of
hate. Some say that God is against us, that He doesn't like us. And
they feel an enormous and crippling sense of rejection and inferiority and resentment.

I tell you that God's quarrel is a *lover's* quarrel. If He had hated
the world, He wouldn't have created it. If He really hated the world,
it wouldn't exist. The truth is that He loved the world into existence, "when the morning stars sang together, and all the sons of
God shouted for joy." It is born in His goodness and sustained
by His mercy. And when it goes wrong, He does not reject it, but
draws near in His Son to put it right. Nobody saw this more clearly
or expressed it more beautifully than the prophet Hosea. He said
that God's quarrel with the world is like that of a man who has a
wife whom he loves deeply but who has been unfaithful to him. He
is brokenhearted about it, but because of his great love for her he
will do everything in his power to win her back.

In the season of Lent, we think of Christ's passion and death.

Do you know what they mean? They mean that God loved us so much that He came to us in Jesus Christ. He joined Himself to us, married us beyond any separation, claiming us as His own. So I conclude with Hosea's great words; it is God's hope — and not only His hope but His greatest accomplishment — that at the last we shall turn to Him and say, "My true husband, my real lover. You are the one to whom I truly belong. You are my eternal home." God has a lover's quarrel with the world, but at the last what remains is not the quarrel, but the love.

PUNCTUATE YOUR LIFE

"In the beginning was the Word . . ."

St. John 1:1

St. Augustine once described himself as "A vendor of words." I suppose preachers could describe themselves as vendors of words. We live by speaking. The uttering of words is a very important part of our vocation. So early in my ministry I decided that if I was going to live by speaking, then every year I would read, or reread, a book of grammar to remind me of how words are used and abused.

I wish that more people who live by words would read books of grammar. I wish, for example, that some of our sports commentators would do so. Have you ever noticed that in football there is never a "third down." There is a "third down situation." Not long ago, in a game I watched, we encountered "a measurement situation." I am not sure how that differs from a measurement, but nowadays everything is a "situation." And then there is Howard Cosell, whom I admire very much. During the Olympics he said that "one boxer threw more punches in terms of number." If you are going to throw more punches, that's the way to do it!

Or think of our weather forecasters. You must have noticed that we never have a shower of rain. We have "intermittent showers." And we never have a thunderstorm. We always have "thunderstorm activity." When I listen to the weather-forecasters, I am relieved that they had nothing to do with the writing of the Bible. If they had, then God would never have said to Noah, "Noah, build yourself an ark because it is going to rain!" He would have said, "Noah, we have to dialogue! There is a flood situation. The scenario weather-wise, as of right now, is a one hundred percent chance of precipitation. And it's going to impact real soon in terms of water."

It may be amusing to talk like this, but there is a dark side to it too. For slovenly speech betrays careless thought. We commonly suppose that speech is the handmaid of thought, but that is not so. As W. H. Auden and others have told us, speech is the mother of thought for thought is a sort of inner speech. The abuse of language reveals confused thinking. And that is why it seems to me that people who are vendors of words ought to read about words.

When you read a book of grammar one of the things you learn about is punctuation; about commas, and full-stops, and all the other punctuation marks. Any writing that is well-punctuated is more coherent and more readily communicated than writing that is not. All of which brings us to the New Testament.

Did you know that the original manuscripts of the New Testament had no punctuation marks? This made the work of translating them much more difficult. The translators constantly had to guess at the meaning in order to know where to put the punctuation marks. And sometimes the placing of a comma was enough to change the sense of a sentence.

While reading books of grammar, I was foolish enough to suppose that punctuation marks are just marks on paper. And then one day I listened to Victor Borge's brilliant and hilarious "Phonetic Punctuation" in which he gives every punctuation mark its own sound. I could make those sounds for you, but most of them are quite rude. It is enough to say that puncutation marks are no longer like small children, to be seen and not heard. Victor Borge's punctuation can be heard!

And then I thought we should go a step further to say that punctuation is not just a matter of writing, or of speaking. It is a matter of living. The well-punctuated life is a life that is more coherent, more meaningful and more readily understood than one that isn't.

So let me ask you: What marks do you need in a well-punctuated life? I am going to mention as many as I have time for, but I hope that you will go on thinking about them and discover others which I have not mentioned.

"Ma" Murray was a remarkable woman from Lillooett, British

Columbia, who for years ran a newspaper. She was much more interested in events than literary style, and people often complained that her newspaper was poorly punctuated. She responded by covering the first page of the first issue of the newspaper in each year with quotation marks, and invited her readers to use them throughout the following months. I am doing something like that this morning. Here are the punctuation marks I think are necessary for the well-punctuated life. Now use them well for the rest of your years!

To begin with, don't you think that the well-punctuated life ought to have question marks in it? Question marks for a sense of wonder, to acknowledge that we don't know everything, and that life is full of mystery.

It was Albert Einstein who said that without a sense of wonder, we might as well be dead. It is the beginning of all true art and science. In other words, he would tell us that astronomy did not begin when somebody tried to see a star or a galaxy through a telescope. It began when someone said, "Twinkle, twinkle, little star, How I *wonder* what you are." Plato knew that. "Wonder at the things around you," he said "for wonder is the beginning of wisdom."

Question marks remind us that our knowledge, however full it may seem, is incomplete and open-ended, and that there is always more to be discovered. This needs to be said because there is an arrogance of mind which assumes that knowledge means the end of mystery. It believes that the more you know the less there is to know. I am inclined to think that the opposite is the truth;that knowledge increases the sense of mystery; that the more you know, the more you know you don't know. I agree with the preacher who used to say, "The larger the island of knowledge, the longer the coastline of mystery."

We need to rediscover a sense of wonder, reverence and humility, for it seems to me that many people who write today do so with an assurance that borders on arrogance. Like the young man in New York who sent his manuscript to a publisher with a covering note which read, "This is only the beginning of my work; the first volume in which I explain the universe." Theresa Greenwood in her *Prayers of a Black Mother* laments for one who has

"Three degrees, but no salvation. Honours, but no honour."

and asks,

"Lord, open the eyes of my boy who has been blinded by a thimblefull of knowledge."

C. Day Lewis talks about the arrogance of some scientists who have been blinded by a thimblefull of knowledge. He has them say,

God is a proposition
And we that prove Him are His priests, His chosen ...
Last week I measured the Light, His little finger,
The rest is a matter of time.

Such people were well described by Oscar Wilde when he said of them that they know the last word about everything and the first word about nothing!

Every Christian ought to know that if God is so small that we can encompass Him with our little minds then He is not great enough to be God. If we can measure Him we have lost Him. Yet some Christians make me uneasy, not because they know too little about God, but because they appear to know too much. They have taken the measure of Him, know His dimensions, and what size of box will contain Him. They can tell us anything about Him that we care to ask, and have a proof-text to answer every question. There is no room for doubt in religion of this sort. Yet doubt is often the cutting edge of faith. It was Unamuno, the great Spanish religious philosopher, who used to say that just as the body uses material substance, food, by turning it into energy and vitality, so doubt is the fuel of faith. The faith that is not punctuated with question marks has lost its energy and vitality.

Life, of course, has a way of humbling us when we grow conceited and think we know so much. It was Harry Truman who said that "it is what you learn after you know it all that really counts." And I chuckle at the story of the young man who had just received his degree and came bursting out of convocation shouting, "Here I am, World; I have a B.A.!" And the World replied, "Stick around, son, and I'll teach you the rest of the alphabet!"

Some years ago, my son studied psychology at the University of Western Ontario. I noticed that one of his text books had yellow pages at the end of every chapter. I discovered that the white pages of the text stated firm conclusions. The yellow pages were much more tentative. They were concerned not so much with giving the right answers as asking the right questions.

Every life should have yellow pages of that sort. Sometimes we try to evade the questions which we find unsettling. They disturb us. But questions are a sign of life and vitality, and every life should have some. A great poet shows us how best to regard them when he says, "Be patient toward all that is unsolved in your heart, and try to love the questions themselves." The well-punctuated life has question marks.

Notice, next, that the well-punctuated life ought to have quotation marks to acknowledge our indebtedness to others.

Blaise Pascal said once that no author should ever refer to "my" book. No one ever wrote a book by himself. Montaigne was even more candid. He wrote, "In this book I have gathered a posie of other men's flowers, and nothing but the thread that binds them is my own."

Now that is very close to the truth, though many of us might not care to admit it. We like to think that we are original thinkers. Have you ever had an original thought? Can you think of one?

I wrote a poem, once. It was a short poem of only four lines, but they were good lines, and I was proud of them. Imagine my astonishment when I came across "my" poem in a book that had been written years before I was born. The explanation was simple. I had read the poem at an earlier time and had forgotten it. But it was still there in the depths of my mind and then, as such thoughts often do, it had worked its way to the surface again as "my" poem. We are far more indebted to others even than we realize.

But quotation marks not only declare our indebtedness; they are the mark of a well-furnished mind. They are the sign of a rich interior life.

Margaret Prescott Montague was an American novelist and short-story writer. From childhood she suffered from progressive blindness and later was menaced by almost total deafness. When she learned that her world was to be a world not only of darkness but of silence as well, she replied, "If the world be shut without, I'll sail the hidden seas within." And for her, "the hidden seas within" were like the great oceans of the world; broad and deep and teeming with life, for her mind was well-furnished. I know others and their "hidden seas" are little more than a duck-pond, muddy and shallow and painfully narrow. They are like the man so well described by Robert Louis Stevenson, who has reached the age of forty and hasn't yet managed two thoughts to rub the one against the other while waiting for a train.

How well-furnished is your mind? Do you enjoy a rich interior life? If you were to be removed from all external stimuli, like so many condemned to solitary confinement in prison, would your inner thoughts be great and varied enough to sustain you? Did you know that John Buchan knew *Pilgrim's Progress* off by heart? I knew a man who said that it would be no loss if all copies of *Paradise Lost* were lost; he could write it out from memory. I know a theologian who had learned by heart every line of Shakespeare's historical plays. Such people remind me of the man in Edgar Frank's poem "Goshen!" A friend asked him how he could live in the wretched country town of Goshen where the people do little more than gossip and plant cabbages. The man replied that he did not live in Goshen. He ate there, slept there, and worked there. But he lived in Greece with Plato, and dwelt in Italy with Dante. A thousand souls had left him enchantment that transcended time and place, and so he lived in Paradise, not Goshen.

I am sure you have often noticed how splendidly furnished our Lord's mind was. George MacDonald once remarked of Him that He never tried to be original. Of course, He *was* original. Other people said of Him, "Never man spake like this man." He has uniquely shown us the heart and mind of the Father. But He did so not by trying to be original, but by steeping Himself in the prophets of Israel and the psalmists, so that when He went into the synagogue at Nazareth He interpreted His life's work in the words of the prophet Isaiah; and when He was tempted of the devil in the wilderness, He overcame him by the power of words written by the psalmist hundreds of years earlier.

Christians, of course, get quotation marks into their lives by filling their minds with the words of Christ. Dr. Fosdick used to say that our Lord lived His life like music to be played over again. We play it over again by remembering what He said and did, and by capturing His loving Spirit. I heard once of a university in the United States which had these words carved over the door of the Department of Philosophy, "Nestle into the mind of Plato, and think from there!" That's very close to the Apostle Paul's exhortation, "Let His mind be in you, which was also in Christ Jesus."

Notice next, the importance of exclamation marks. For our enthusiasms!

The New Testament is full of exclamation marks and it shows us that Jesus was invariably on the side of enthusiasts. The people He found it hardest to take were the cold fish who never got excited about anything.

Do you remember how He entered Jerusalem to the singing of children and the shouts of the crowd? This upset the old scribes and pharisees who urged Him to tell the little ones to shut up. But he didn't. Instead He replied that if the children were quiet, the very stones would cry out!

Are there enthusiasms in your life? Not long ago I read a book called *The Enthusiasms of Robertson Davies*. I loved it! His enthusiasms range all the way from Mozart to figgy-pudding. Do you have any enthusiasms? Schweitzer once warned us that life steals them. Hector Berlioz remarked that when young we should lay in a vast store of them, for the passing years will rob us of them. Has that happened to you? I read that Eugene Ormandy dislocated his shoulder while conducting the Philadelphia orchestra. I wonder what he was playing. Brahms, perhaps. In the margin of one of his symphonies Brahms wrote, "As loud as possible!" And a few bars later, "Louder still!" I know some people who have reached middle-age and have never had an enthusiasm great enough to dislocate their necktie let alone their shoulder.

Did you hear of the little girl whose grandmother was ill, and whose minister asked her how her grandmother was? The little girl replied gravely that her grandmother had unfortunately lapsed into a comma. That has happened to more people than her grandmother!

Just as it is the purpose of education to teach us to admire what is truly admirable, to appreciate what *ought* to be appreciated, so it is one function of religious faith to give us enthusiasms which are worthy of us. The New Testament is full of them, and behind every one there is an exclamation mark. Rise! Shine! Fear Not! Courage! Mark's gospel especially has more than its share. The church seems to have lost some of them. We have reduced the good news of the gospel to mere morality, and the celebration of faith to the performance of a duty, and who ever got excited about duty or mere morality? I know churches that are dying from a sense of duty. They lack the charm, graciousness, and joy of a great enthusiasm. And as Dick Shepherd used to say, such churches deserve to have their roof torn off.

When Mother Teresa finally decided to allow the BBC to film her work among the dying in Calcutta she said to Malcolm Muggeridge, "Malcolm, let's do it! Let's do something beautiful for God!" And her enthusiasm derives from this, that she does what she does, not for a reason, but for a person, and that is where all the joy comes in, and so she does it as beautifully as she can. Wrote Charles Wesley in one of his great hymns, "My heart it doth dance at the sound of His name." Don't trust a religion that doesn't end in a doxology!

Question marks for mystery. Quotation marks for indebtedness. Exclamation marks for our enthusiasms. Notice, next, that the well-punctuated life knows what to underline.

Underlining must be used sparingly. The emphasis should be carried in the vocabulary and style, so that it should not be necessary to underline much. We must not be like Queen Victoria who in her diaries underlined everything. She must have thought that everything she said was important. But, of course, if you underline everything you might as well underline nothing. Occasionally, though, it is useful to underline a word here or there. For particular emphasis.

Many of my books are secondhand. In bookseller's jargon the more expensive ones are "pre-owned". The most expensive ones are "pre-appreciated"! One of the enjoyable things about them is that sometimes the previous owners have underlined sentences here and there. The bits they thought important. The fun of it is in agreeing or disagreeing with their judgment, and carrying on a conversation with them to confirm or contest their insight.

Coventry Patmore, the poet, was married several times. When he met a woman in whom he had a romantic interest, he would lend her a fresh copy of his favourite book and invite her to underline the parts she thought important. When she returned the book he would scrutinize the parts she had underlined. If he agreed with her judgment the affair went forward; if he didn't, it didn't!

Every life underlines something, emphasizes some values, believes some things to be more important than others. There is a close relationship between underlining and worship. To worship means to ascribe worth. Worship is worth-ship. And, of course, you ascribe worth to the things that are important to you, to the things you underline. One of the functions of religion is to help us to ascribe worth to the things that are worthy. To underline the right things.

William Temple once remarked that the world is like a shop window full of articles. But someone has slipped in and mischievously mixed up the price-tags, so that some valuable goods are priced cheaply, and some shoddy merchandise has a high price-tag. The New Testament teaches us the importance of underlining the right things, thereby helping us to express a true sense of values. It exhorts us to seek *first* the Kingdom of God. It tells us the *greatest* commandment, which is to love God. Are you underlining the right things, and expressing a true sense of values?

Here is another bit of advice from the grammar books that can be helpful in life. They tell us to enclose parentheses between brackets. In this way we see that parentheses can be inserted or taken out without interrupting the flow of the sentence, or the tale that is being told. They are interludes, briefly stated and soon over. The story goes on.

Every life has parentheses, and the well-punctuated life knows how to recognize them and what to do with them. Sometimes we call them holidays. Or retreats. Or sabbaticals. They are intervals taken out of the busyness of our days, for our refreshment. And most lives at one time or other have unhappy interludes. People experience sorrow, or grief, or loneliness. The important thing is to recognize them for what they are, and to believe that we shall pass through them. The well-punctuated life recognizes a parenthesis when it sees one, and knows that it is not a settled, continuing state.

A good name for such parentheses is "wilderness experiences." The Hebrew word for wilderness means "a place to pass through." I once passed through the Judean wilderness in an air-conditioned bus. I made no attempt to *stay* in the wilderness. It is too dangerous. Bishop James Pike and his wife parked their car on the road which goes through the wilderness of Judea, and wandered a few yards into the desert. He never found his way back. He perished in the wilderness, and his wife nearly did.

I know some people who dwell in their wilderness experiences instead of passing through them, and they perish there. They dwell in a wilderness of guilt, or fear, or anxiety, or inferiority. Make your own list of wilderness experiences, and notice how many of your friends are dwelling in them when they ought to be passing through them. You may be doing so yourself! Some people have the idea that the Christian faith has some sort of vested interest in having people dwell in guilt and inferiority. It is not so! The loving intention of God is that guilt should be swallowed up in His forgiveness; and fear, inferiority and anxiety should become faith, trust, and confidence.

It can be a great help to notice that so many of our wilderness experiences are parentheses. They don't last forever. Nathaniel Hawthorne said that it was one of the greatest of all mortal consolations that we can say of so many dark experiences, "This, too, shall pass."

If that is true, then one of the most valuable lessons we can learn is that waiting is a kind of doing. Sometimes the waiting is all that we can manage, and all that can be expected of us. Getting the hours in is victory of a sort. In the lovely words of Robert Louis Stevenson, we can "win through till nightfall," and that is accomplishment enough.

Parentheses of this sort remind me of a boxer who has taken a heavy punch, so that the only thing he can do is hang on till the end of the round. There is no glory in hanging on. It means that you are playing for time, getting the seconds in until your head clears and you can catch your breath. Some of life's experiences are like that. To get the time in is as much as you can manage. And it is the difference between victory and defeat.

Have you seen an Irish Round Tower? The tower points like a

pencil to the sky, and they all have a door high above the ground. The Round Tower was a means of survival when the Irish were attacked by hostile people (mostly the Scots!). They kept the tower stocked with food, and when the enemy appeared they entered the high door by a ladder, pulled the ladder up inside the tower, closed the heavy door and waited for the marauders to go home. Sometimes they swore at them in Gaelic, which is a marvellous language for swearing!

Some experiences in life are like that. We get through them because we know they will pass. We get the hours in. And waiting is a kind of doing. Remember it!

Here is another piece of punctuation I want to mention. One book of grammar says, "Form the possessive singular of nouns by adding the apostrophe 's'." In other words, the well-punctuated life must know how to deal wisely with its possessions.

Some people talk about *my* time, *my* talents, *my* money. When they talk like that they often live like that. They become narrow and selfish, so that their possessions begin to possess them.

Ernest Hemingway used to give things away at the beginning of a new year. He said he did so to prove that he owned them. If he couldn't give them away, he didn't own them, they owned him. And he lamented that we spend so much attention on things that cannot feel and cannot love instead of lavishing our care on people who can feel our affection and return our love.

C. S. Lewis loved books. Someone once asked him if there would be books in heaven. He replied that the only books in our heavenly libraries would be the ones we had given to others. "Nothing that you have not given away will ever be really yours," he said. Our Lord believed this to be true not only of the things we possess in life, but of life itself. It was He who told us that to have life we must be willing to lose it; to truly possess it we must fling it away.

Listen! What if *being* is more important than having? What if what you are is more important than anything you possess? What if, in the end, you can't give me anything I can keep, except love? What if power and possessions are only means of loving or not loving? What if, in the end, Caesar's share really is only a penny, and you bear the image of God?

Well, that would turn life upside down, wouldn't it? Rudyard Kipling once spoke to the graduating students of McGill University in Montreal. He looked at them, all bright-eyed and bushy-tailed; all going out to gain the whole world; some of them after power, and some after fame, and some after money and security. He said to them, "One day you are going to meet a man who cares for none of these things, and you will envy him!" We have met some men like that. And some women, too. Supremely we have met one Man like that. But we do not envy Him. We adore Him, and call ourselves by His name!

Yet another book of grammar tells us our last rule of punctuation. "Make the paragraph the unit of composition," it says. Not the page. Not the chapter. The paragraph! You recognize the wisdom of that, for you know what it is like to see solid pages of black type in front of you, page after page, dense and discouraging. It needs to be broken up, made more lightsome, with dialogue and frequent divisions so that it *looks* attractive and encourages us to read.

The well-punctuated life is like that! Viscount Grey, who carried enormous responsibilities in the first world war, was once asked how he came through it all. He said that he was able to do it because he refused to live life in the lump. That's a good phrase! Some of us are trying to live life in the lump and it is proving too much for us. We heap up responsibilities, and obligations, and demands. We worry about tomorrow today. And about next week this week. We carry what someone has called, "An overweight of worry." So it crushes us. We need to make the paragraph the unit of composition, and break up our life into manageable portions.

When Eric Sevareid was seventeen years old, he and a school buddy decided to paddle a canoe from Minneapolis to Hudsons Bay. The worst stretch was four hundred and fifty miles of river, with much white water and with only one settlement. Before they started on their journey they met an old fur trapper who gave them a bit of advice. He told them to think only of the next mile. He warned them never to think of the mile after that, and never, never, of the four hundred and fifty miles.

I know all kinds of people who can't manage their lives because they are always thinking of the four hundred and fifty miles. They try to carry tomorrow's burdens with today's strength, and the burden proves too much for them and they break down. If, taking our Lord's advice, they would allow one day's troubles to be enough for the day, they could win through to nightfall. The psalmist put it clearly, "As thy days, so shall thy strength be." Troubles come one day at a time, and that is how strength is given and received.

What would life be like if it were not divided up into youth, middle-age, and old age? If we didn't have silver, and then golden anniversaries? If we didn't have Christmas in December, and summer holidays in July, and Thanksgiving in the Fall? If we didn't have decades, and years, and weeks and days, and morning, noon and night? And what would it be like if we couldn't see the end from the beginning? William Morris once said that the whole charm of existence is our mortality; life is wonderful because it does not go on forever. I believe it! I think I can cope with seventy or eighty or even ninety years; but how could one cope with a thousand? I couldn't get a grip on that. But I can grasp the Bible's three-score years and ten, and perhaps a little more. I can divide that up and make it manageable.

And then I remember that our whole life on earth is just a little part of our true life, for we belong to the Eternal. We are nurslings of immortality. Our Lord told us that in heaven there are many resting-places, and the word means inns along the way, so that even there, as here, our pilgrimage is manageable, and the journey will not overwhelm us.

And now I'm going to slip in one punctuation mark more than I promised. It is the period, the full-stop. All books come to an end. Every well-punctuated life should know when to use the full-stop. This is especially true of preachers.

SECRET DISCIPLES

"Pilate was approached by Joseph of Arimathea, a disciple of Jesus, but a secret disciple for fear of the Jews, who asked to be allowed to remove the body of Jesus ... He was joined by Nicodemus (the man who had first visited Jesus by night)."

St. John 19:38,39

Our text from St. John's gospel tells us about two men who came to Pilate and asked if they might have the body of Jesus. Pilate gave his consent and the two men took the body away and buried it. One of the men was Joseph of Arimathea of whom the gospel says that he was a disciple of Jesus, "but secretly, for fear of the Jews." The second man was Nicodemus, "the same who first came to Jesus by night."

Those words fire my imagination. What a human interest story! Joseph of Arimathea, who hardly appears in the Scriptures at all; and Nicodemus who is referred to only three times. He is "Nicodemus who came to Jesus by night"; he is mentioned as defending Christ at an early meeting of the Jewish Council; and he is the man who on this last occasion provided the precious ointment to anoint the body of our Lord. Secret disciples! Joseph of Arimathea, a disciple of Jesus, but secretly; and Nicodemus, who first came to Jesus by night.

The Greek philosopher Epictetus, a Stoic, once said that everything has two handles. By one handle you can carry it; by the other you cannot. He gives us an instance of what he means. If your brother offends you, you cannot carry the relationship by the handle of the offence. If you brood on the offence, the estrangement between you and your brother will grow. But you can carry it by reminding yourself that the man is your brother. Carry the estrangement by the handle of your brotherhood and you have some hope of reconciliation.

Now we have two handles by which to carry the secret discipleship of Joseph and Nicodemus. By which handle shall we carry it? Some people carry this story by the handle of secrecy. They are critical of Joseph and Nicodemus. They make their secrecy a shameful thing and see the men as cowards. This harsh judgment of the secret disciples shows us ourselves in a favourable light. We come to Christ openly, in the full brightness of day. One of them stole to Him secretly, by night, and the other kept his discipleship a secret, from fear.

I think that such a comparison is mistaken and unfair. For one thing, is our discipleship as open as we claim? That is a good question for us to ask ourselves. If we reflect on it we may conclude that we are not different from Joseph and Nicodemus. Our discipleship is more often hidden than we suppose, and we have less justification than Joseph and Nicodemus. To profess discipleship was for them a far more dangerous thing than it is for us. If we knew that our profession of faith might cost us what theirs could have cost them, we'd be less confident of our courage and regard theirs with greater respect.

"The Inklings" were a group of scholars at Oxford who regularly met for conversation and companionship. They met in a pub called "The Eagle and the Child" but known colloquially as "The Bird and Baby." It was there that C. S. Lewis first read to the Inklings *The Screwtape Letters*, and J. R. R. Tolkien first read *The Hobbit*. They met through the decade of the thirties, including the anxious months when it seemed that a German invasion of Britain was imminent. In light of that, they resolved to go through all their writings to discover how much of their work would be condemned by the Nazis. They did this, not from cowardice but from curiosity, to determine which writings would declare their Christianity against the encroaching darkness of fascism.

It's a good exercise for all of us. How secret is our discipleship? If we were to be accused in a court of law of being a Christian, would there be enough evidence to convict us? Well, would there? Would our children testify that we discussed the faith at home? Would our co-workers testify that we were known for our religious beliefs at work? There are people who, if they were charged with being members of this congregation, would be acquitted because the evidence would be insufficient to convict them. Yet their names are on our church roll. Some of them come at Easter and some at Christmas. They remind me of the man who complained that his church was really in a rut, because every time he went there they had a Christmas tree. Some people pay more in green-fees at the country club than they give to the work of the church. Some have more regular encounters with crab grass than they have with Sunday worship. A court of law would have to give them the benefit of the doubt. They could never be convicted of being church members. So remember that we are not different from Nicodemus and Joseph of Arimathea. We are often secret disciples too. If we are disciples at all!

One of the differences between them and us is that they had better reasons for their secrecy. For one thing, they were members of the Sanhedrin, the Supreme Jewish Council of seventy-one members. Joseph and Nicodemus were influential members. They were powerful men; wealthy, responsible, and conservative. They wouldn't have been on the Sanhedrin if they had been radicals. For men such as these, a wandering Galilean with a popular following was someone to be considered carefully. So they were right to be cautious. There are some people in the New Testament who were easily carried this way and that way by the changing winds of doctrine. Not Joseph of Arimathea, and not Nicodemus! They were more responsible than that. They had colleagues in the inner circle who had confided in them and who trusted them. They were not young men; they were mature and set in their ways. Like you and me, they did not find it easy to change their ideas and their way of doing things. Nicodemus was to discover that. Changing his ideas required a travail like childbirth. The very idea of it perplexed and bewildered him. The invitation of our Lord to Nicodemus to become as a little child was not trival. It asked him to revolutionize his thinking; to take his most basic ideas and turn them upside down; to transform what he used to stand for into ideas and allegiances of which he had been wary and suspicious. That was no small adjustment! It was like a new birth!

No wonder Nicodemus and Joseph were cautious. Here was this young Galilean who invited their trust. They had longed for and expected the Kingdom of God. Now here was a young man who said that He was it; that the Kingdom of God was present in Him. But He offered no guarantees. Some people asked Him for a sign, and He replied, "There is no sign given!" He was Himself the sign! How could He give them a sign when He was Himself the reality to which the sign could only point? They had to make up their minds about *Him*.

The longer I live the more convinced I become that the real enemy of faith is not doubt, but fear. Doubt is not the enemy of faith but a lively element in faith, its cutting edge by which we learn and grow. The real enemy is fear. It is not that we are afraid of anyone, but we are afraid of being deceived, looking foolish, giving our trust to those who may not be worthy of it, appearing to be inconsistent. We are so afraid that we refuse to think new thoughts, and we become so careful and set in our ways that we are hemmed in by anxiety and timidity.

Indeed, the real enemy of faith is not even sin, but fear. That may sound surprising, but it is what one gathers from the New Testament. Dr. Frederick Greaves once wrote a book about sin in which he counted the number of occasions, allowing for duplication in the various Gospels, on which Jesus mentioned sin. Greaves discovered that He used the noun six times and the verb three times. But Bishop Stephen Neil tells of a very methodical German scholar who went through the Scriptures and discovered that ninety-nine times the words "Fear not!" echo and re-echo throughout the Bible. What wrought the change in Joseph and Nicodemus was that by dying for them our Lord showed them a love that they could trust, even with their fears. And when they did trust, they found their courage, and no longer secret disciples, they came openly and asked Pilate for the body of Jesus.

Can we allow that same love to overcome our caution and set us free? Can we also be delivered from the fears that inhibit us, and hem us in, and smother our spirit? Can we also be "set in a large place," which is what the word salvation means?

We have noticed that some people try to carry these secret disciples by the handle of secrecy and as a result put Joseph and Nicodemus down. What a pity! The two men deserve better of us. Nor does our poor treatment of them stop there. Some people see Joseph of Arimathea as the epitome of what is meant by the maxim, "too little, too late." Joseph exemplifies, for them, the person who is always intending to visit an old friend until he reads his friend's death notice in the paper; the person who intends to send flowers but waits so long to do it that finally the only place to send them is the funeral home. Joseph embodies all the vain regret we feel over things that we might have done but didn't do. Joseph missed out on Christ's ministry, all the excitement and joy and companionship, and then came along when it was all over to claim the body. "The pity of it!" we say, "To claim a dead body when he could have responded to the claims of the Lord of life!" But again, let's not make Joseph of Arimathea a different species, because in this matter also he is just like you and me.

I don't know anyone who does not live with some kind of vain regret. I have never yet conducted a funeral service at which the mourners did not have a deep sense not only of sorrow but of remorse. Invariably we punish ourselves by saying, "If only I had done this" or "I might have done that" or "I did not do enough." This predicament is as old as life and death and the instances of it are legion.

You remember how when Samuel Johnson started on his monumental task of compiling the first comprehensive dictionary of the English language he approached Lord Chesterfield, seeking his support? Chesterfield spurned him. Years later, when the great project had been completed and the dictionary was published, Chesterfield tried to claim that he had been Johnson's patron. Johnson would have none of it, and he composed a celebrated letter, a magnificent rebuke, in which he asks rhetorically, "Is not a patron, my Lord, one who looks with unconcern on a man struggling for life in the water, and when he has reached ground encumbers him with help? The notice which you have been pleased to take of my labours, had it been early, had been kind; but it has been delayed 'til I am indifferent, and cannot enjoy it; 'til I am solitary, and cannot impart it; 'til I am known, and do not want it."

"Had it been early, it had been kind!" Isn't that our story? So much that we want to do we leave until it is too late and it remains undone. If you love somebody, tell them now! Don't wait! Let them know! I think again of Samuel Johnson. He was not only the victim of vain regret, he was the author of it. I see him in my mind's eye, standing in the rain in the marketplace at Uttoxeter, an old man with a bowed head, in an act of contrition for the things that he had refused to do as a young man to assist his father. So it goes on, in your life and in my life, the old regrets gnawing away at us and whispering, "too little, too late!" What do we say about this? Let me suggest two or three things.

First, if you insist on playing the game of vain regret, you should realize at the outset that it is a game you cannot win. No matter how kind you were, you could always have been kinder. No matter how generous, you could have given more. So live in vain regret if you must, but do not expect health or sanity or peace of mind or spirit. The game is endless and profitless and incompatible with your happiness. And it denies the fundamental truth of our deepest relationships.

The truth about relationships with loved ones is that they depend not on what we have done or left undone, but on what we are. My children are the meaning of my life, not because of anything they do for me, but simply because they are mine and I love them. That love is the meaning of my life and my love for them is their supreme gift to me. And that love does not depend on a careful reckoning of what they have done, or left undone, or of what they might have done. Such a view would trivialize the relationship. And so it is with you and your relationships. Of course you could have done more. But it isn't important. The important thing is that you lived and loved and were loved. You gave meaning to someone else's life. That is enough. You are not perfect. No one is. All of us live by grace. The marvellous thing is that those vain regrets can be turned into instruments of humility and compassion and understanding when we realize that we are all imperfect and live by the mercy of God and of others. We are forgiven. When we live in the light of our having been forgiven, rather than in the shadow of regret, we experience the joy and the openness to other people that comes from it; what the New Testament calls, "the glorious liberty of the children of God." Of course we have regrets, because we are not perfect. But we also know the joy that comes from being loved and being forgiven.

Here is another thing to notice. It is that God takes the dark side of our life, even the vain regret, and uses it to make us what we are.

That's something to hold on to. Not the regrets, but the grace that can do so much with even the dark side of our life. Take Saul of Tarsus who became Paul the Apostle! What regrets he must have had! He persecuted the Christian church. If that is not enough to haunt the wee small hours of the morning then what is? Yet that is not what Paul dwells on. He mentions it, but goes on at once to write this marvellous sentence, "Nevertheless, by the grace of God, I am what I am." That is the handle by which St. Paul carried his past. Not by regret or by guilt, though there was plenty of both, but by the providence of God which is an inexhaustible power to bring good out of evil.

I say to those who carry Joseph of Arimathea and Nicodemus by the handle of their secretiveness, you unjustly disparage them. They deserve better treatment. I tell you that there is another handle, a marvellous one, by which to carry them. Even though they were secret disciples, nevertheless by the grace of God they were disciples. They were disciples secretly, but disciples nevertheless.

Now I must tell you, in all honesty, that I sometimes wish our discipleship were a little more secret. When I read a headline in the paper, as I did the other day, saying that a United Church Conference supported a resolution approving civil disobedience, but didn't find any specific case in which the resolution might be applied, then I wish that our discipleship were more secret. That seemed to me to be an extraordinarily foolish and timid ending to such a brave headline. I found it disturbing, because such bravado is too easy. It costs us nothing. There is no country in the world, I suppose, in which it is easier to pass a resolution like that than our own. Nobody suffered! What empty courage! What brave mouths! What hollow heroism! Not long ago I shared a broadcast with a young man, a radical theologian, who quoted the *Magnificat* to me and said that it was a radical document calling for nothing less than a revolution in society's structures and values. That disturbed me too, for it cost him nothing to say it. He assumed a position of moral ascendancy, and breathed an atmosphere of moral heroism unwarranted by any action he had taken. His position and his salary were secure, and when the television programme was over, he returned to his tenured professorship. Yet the implication was that he was a radical Christian and I was not. It was just words, cheap talk.

Now let me be quite clear about this. I have unbounded admiration for the courage of people who will say those same words and will pay the price of saying them. But I have no respect for the facile eloquence that mouths brave words and then leaves the television studio, climbs into the car, and cheerily drives home afterwards. It is my perception that those who talk most about pain seldom feel it; and those who speak most about risk seldom take one. Or they are prepared to risk someone else's faith, not their own. So I say to you that sometimes I wish our discipleship were more secret, or at least more decently reticent. Carlyle Marney, that tough old American preacher, used to say that a true church will be known because it will be the centre of people's lives. It won't need to advertise. People will discern the truth and the word will get around. It's very hard to hide authentic faith that puts its life where its mouth is.

But I want to go a bit further than that. You see, today is Pentecost. Do you know what Pentecost means? It means the work of the Holy Spirit. It means God working inwardly and secretly in human life to accomplish His loving purpose. Pentecost is a time to remember that all our neat divisions between those who are disciples and those who are not, between those who are saved and those who are unsaved, those who are in and those who are out, all become meaningless before this marvellous, mysterious, secret Spirit of God whose work never ceases in any human heart. So that in every place and at all times in history there are secret disciples acting in response to this same secret Spirit. There are several senses in which this is true. For example, it is true in the sense that no one can live in this world without being influenced by Jesus Christ. They may not claim to be His disciples. Yet if to be a disciple means to learn, then it is inevitable that they learn of Him because our society has been shaped by Him. Our institutions, our laws, morals, literature, art, music, all demonstrate that. You can't even write the date on a letter without acknowledging Him. We date our centuries from His coming. So it is that even in a society where many deny Him, or are unaware of Him, it is impossible to live as though He never lived. No one can advance the most superficial claim to be educated who does not know the Christian faith. Apart from it, one cannot understand Shakespeare, or interpret Vaughan Williams' music, or make sense of any art gallery or museum. And yet one hears foolish talk of teaching morality without religion. How can it be done? Every moral decision that we make, the very discourse of moral judgement, derives from and is illumined by words once spoken by the Lake of Galilee. So today when I hear young people claiming to have rejected Christianity in favour of Buddhism or Hinduism or some religion of the Far East, I find it little less than frivolous. Why should young men and women who have been shaped by this Christian culture, who were born into it, nurtured and brought up in it, search anywhere but in Him for the challenge of a faith to live by?

Notice, too, that there are some who are secret disciples because they don't know they are disciples. They are far more Christian than they realize. Examples of this crowd my mind. I think of Malcolm Muggeridge who, in his sixties, wrote a celebrated book called *Jesus Rediscovered*. But if you read Muggeridge's early writings in an anthology called *Things Past* compiled by my friend Professor Ian Hunter, you discover that there is a sense in which Muggeridge always was a Christian. He didn't know he was, but from the beginning his writing was infused with an appreciation of Christian values and the inexhaustible enchantment of Christ. To the discerning eye, the truth and beauty of the Christian faith, and the unfailing attraction of Jesus Christ, were his themes from the very beginning. A secret disciple! Something similar might be said about Bertrand Russell and many others as well. Russell saw himself as the enemy of faith, and opposed Christianity at every opportunity. First-year university students still read his superficial essay, "Why I am Not a Christian." Yet his own daughter in her biographical sketch of her father says, "He was by temperament a profoundly religious man ... I believe myself that his whole life was a search for God." Unbeknownst, even to themselves, there are secret disciples.

Let me say something more. We ought to recognize that because this universal Spirit of God works universally, there are many people of other religions who are secret disciples of Christ, for they have His Spirit. I read the other day of a Christian who had been treated kindly by a Jewish friend. Without thinking he turned to his friend and said, "That was a very Christian thing to do." Instantly, his friend replied, "Yes, it was also a very Jewish thing to do." So often we look for differences between religious faiths and we use the differences to show that one is superior. Don't you think it might be a good thing if we looked instead for the stirrings and the murmurings of that Spirit of God who works in all faiths and in all people? The reiterated message of the New Testament is that the Spirit will not be restricted to our neat divisions and systems, but in His sovereign freedom confounds all the limitations we set for Him.

My old teacher, Professor E. L. Allen, a distinguished theologian and missionary, told me once that he never went into a village in China thinking that he was bringing Christ to the people for the first time. In a sense he was, for he preached the gospel in places where it had never been preached before. But he told me that he always arrived to find that Christ was there already, present by His Spirit in the hearts of all. I love the story of the old Hindu woman who said to a missionary from whom she first heard the gospel, "Thank you! I have always loved Him and now you have told me His name."

There is one last way in which our discipleship is secret. It is that your influence and mine is often a secret influence. We seldom know what our own influence is, and it is easy to underestimate it and to grow discouraged. When I tell you that I have never had more confidence in what I preach than I have today, it is a confidence that does not arise out of conceit or arrogance. It is simply that the response is out of all proportion to the stimulus. It is because God takes our little mustard-seed of faith, and the poor words that we speak, and works miracles with them in other hearts and lives. Do you understand what I am saying? I am saying that the making of Christians is far more God's work than it is yours or mine. Thank God for that, because we are not much good at it. What a comfort and relief it is to know that he will take the feeble effort which is all we have to give and somehow use it to accomplish His loving purpose. The marvel of grace is not merely that He accomplishes His purpose in an imperfect world, but that He does so with such imperfect instruments.

Secret disciples! Dear friend, we are all secret disciples. Fosdick once complained about people who look better than they really are. They are not as Christian as they seem. Then he went on to say, "Yes, but we owe others the obligation to seem as Christian as we are! Not to hide our light under a bushel. To believe that God will take and use what we have and what we are to be of strength and healing to others."

Let me finish with a story, an apocryphal one. Many legends surround the name of Joseph of Arimathea. Several of them link him to England. There is one, for example, which says that Joseph of Arimathea was a tin merchant who frequently visited the tin mines of Cornwall, and once brought the Christ-child with him. There is another which tells how, after the resurrection, the disciples gave Joseph of Arimathea the chalice which had held the wine at the last supper, because he had given Jesus a tomb. The legend is that in the year A.D. 61 Joseph of Arimathea came to England to preach the gospel and brought the chalice with him, and that he buried it in the English hills. Later in his life, when Joseph was an old man, the glorified Christ came and walked with him in the evening through the English countryside.

Legends! Why do I trouble you with legends? Why do I bother to tell you of the pre-eminence of *Saint* Joseph Arimathea in Glastonbury, England? My reason is that because of him we have a gift of inspiration. It was William Blake who heard this old legend of how Joseph of Arimathea and the glorified Christ walked together on England's hills and it so moved Blake that he wrote his poem, *Jerusalem.* One who was a disciple, but secretly for fear of the Jews, gives to you and to me the strength of faith through the gift of praise. Here are Blake's words:

And did those feet in ancient time,
Walk upon England's mountains green?
And was the holy Lamb of God
On England's pleasant pastures seen?
And did the countenance divine
Shine forth upon our clouded hills?
And was Jerusalem builded here
Among these dark, satanic mills?

Bring me my bow of burning gold:
Bring me my arrows of desire:

Bring me my spear, O clouds unfold!
Bring me my chariots of fire.
I will not cease from mental fight
Nor shall my sword sleep in my hand,
Till we have built Jerusalem
In England's green and pleasant land.

Thank you, Joseph of Arimathea, Secret Disciple!

FUNDAMENTAL FALLACIES

"When in former times God spoke to our forefathers, He spoke in fragmentary and varied fashion through the prophets. But in this the final age He has spoken to us in His son."

Hebrews 1:1

I confess a real sense of concern at the resurgence of conservative religion, specifically fundamentalism and the biblical literalism it preaches. If you watch television, you cannot avoid it. The media ministers are on it all the time. My concern is that what they say is often a distortion of the message of Scripture.

Fundamentalism presents a mistaken view of the nature of the Bible. Inevitably, it presents us with an inadequate, and sometimes even an un-Christian, idea of God. In pastoral counselling I talk frequently to people who have suffered great anguish of mind and spirit because of the cruel and vindictive motives and actions which such a view imputes to our Heavenly Father.

Another concern I have is that intelligent people who watch such programmes are repelled. They may think that this is the only kind of Christianity there is. Well, if that were so, then I would not be a Christian. If we believe that the Christian truth we hold is vital and alive and enriching, then let us apply it to fundamentalism and see what we discover. I have four criticisms to offer.

The first thing to notice about fundamentalists or Bible literalists is that while they say the Bible is true, they narrow the truth that the Bible is.

The fundamentalist view of truth is too cribbed and confined. Truth, for them, is what is literally, scientifically, and historically true. Now that is too narrow a view of truth for me. But if we don't accept the narrow definition of truth which the literalists offer us, then they condemn us by declaring that we do not believe the Bible.

Consider, for example, the doctrine of creation. The fundamentalists say that in Genesis the Bible teaches that God made the world in six days and rested on the seventh. They take this literally. To them it is a scientific statement of fact. And, of course, inevitably, it comes into conflict with other scientific statements about creation. So immediately we have a tension between a six day creation which the literalists say the Bible teaches, and the theory of evolution which most scientists, indeed most modern people, believe. With the conflict come absurd spectacles like the infamous Scopes trial in Dayton, Tennessee, with champions on each side — Darrow vs. Bryan — brandishing their holy writ — Genesis vs. Darwin — in contests which produce a lot of heat and smoke but very little light.

Now notice that if we hold that Genesis is literally true, that creation occurred in six days, then we have some serious difficulties to answer. Do you know that in the first two chapters of Genesis we have not one account of creation but two? Did you know that? In one account man is created at the beginning; in the other account he is created at the end. If this is a scientific statement, what are we to make of it? How are we to reconcile the two accounts? If Genesis is scientific then we must believe that God made night and day before He created the sun. But how could such an account be taken seriously as a bit of science? Nevertheless, if Genesis is a scientific account, that's what we have to believe. Do you believe that?

The trouble with the creation-evolution debate is that both sides are tempted to impose a twentieth-century scientific world view upon people who wrote thousands of years ago. Do you know how recent what we would consider a modern scientific world view really is? It is not older than three centuries. Yet those who look for science in Genesis impose this world view on those who, thousands of years ago, wrote the first chapters of the Bible.

I believe that the Book of Genesis is not scientific in any sense. There is simply no science in Genesis. The authors of the splendid accounts of creation in the Book of Genesis knew little about how the world was created. They knew even less about the nature of the universe in which we live. Not only did they know little about the scientific view, I suspect they cared little about it. They were not interested. They never tried to give us a little science. They attempted to give us a great deal of religion. And they gave us a book full of profound spiritual and moral insight.

The plain fact is that the writers of Genesis were not interested in *how* the world was created. They were preoccupied with a far more difficult and important question: *Why* was it created? They were not interested in what happened when, and how; they were passionately interested in why, and in the moral and spiritual relations which the answer to that question revealed: God's relations with His world; Man's relations with God; Man's relations with his brother. The writers were poets, not scientists, and as poets they not only contemplated the magnitude of God's creation but felt His fingers shaping their own life to the divine likeness. In praise and awe, they shouted aloud that this God, who created them, who called them from this round earth's imagined corners into life and being, had created everything in which their life and being was grounded. You see, to create me, God had to make a universe; for to give me life He had to create everything from which my life is made, the soil and the stars, the wind and the moon, the trees and the rain.

> What does it take to make a rose, mother mine?
> It takes the world's eternal wars.
> It takes the moon and all the stars.
> It takes the might of heaven and hell.
> And the Everlasting Love as well, little child.

Now that is a spiritual insight. It is profound and it is true. But it has nothing to do with science. So both the creationists and the evolutionists who go to the Bible for scientific support are equally mistaken. Because you won't find any science there. That is not the kind of book it is.

Another example of the distortion produced by biblical literalism is the Book of Jonah. What a marvellous book it is, so full of humour and pathos! But you must understand that it is not a literal account of something that actually happened. God is not more limited than we are in how He speaks; and we communicate not only through literal truth, but through poetry, symbols, parables, fiction, allegory, satire, and in many other literary forms. God is not limited to the prosaic matter-of-fact prose to which the fundamentalists want to tie Him down.

The Book of Jonah was written when racial exclusivism was dominant in Israel. Many Jews believed that God loved them and nobody else. They believed that He existed in their territory but was not concerned about any other country or nation. Along came Jonah, sent to preach to the people of Nineveh. Nineveh was a foreign city, full of gentile unbelievers, people for whom the exclusivists declared that God had no care. The prospect of preaching to them was so distasteful to Jonah that he tried to escape it by fleeing from God. He discovered that it is impossible to escape from God for there is nowhere else to go. At last, and reluctantly, he returned to preach to the people of Nineveh. A marvellous thing happened. They not only listened; they repented! God had mercy on them! How did Jonah feel about that? He was outraged! So disappointed was he that God should have mercy on such people that he wanted to die. Then God came to Jonah and said, "Jonah, can't you understand that I love the people of Nineveh, as I love you and all the people of Israel? Can you not share my pity for them, and understand my compassion? Jonah, don't you see that my care is all-encompassing?"

What a marvellous story it is, full of insight and truth. It speaks of the universalism of God's grace and it is a preparation for the coming of our Lord and the universal faith of the New Testament. So what have we done with Jonah? The Bible literalists say, "Look, this is history! If you don't believe that this is literally and scientifically and historically true, then you don't believe the Bible!" So this marvellous story is reduced to just one hoary old question, "Do you think a whale swallowed Jonah, and that he could live for three days and nights in its belly, and survive?" That is the issue. Many people do not know what the Book of Jonah is about — the story of God's universal saving grace. But everyone knows about Jonah and the whale. It becomes a stumbling block, instead of a guidepost, to faith. A fundamentalist once remarked, "If it said so in the Bible, I would believe not only that the whale swallowed Jonah but that Jonah swallowed the whale!" That really does him no credit. When you look for a wee tiny bit of historical truth, you might miss a great spiritual truth. Jonah isn't history. But it's a marvellous bit of truth. As someone said, the whale has become a red herring! Surely we can see that the spiritual insight and power of the story does not depend on its being literally true.

Now this example we have chosen serves to illustrate for us the great variety of ways in which God reveals Himself to us. Suppose I were to bring together a number of books in an anthology. Let's see: We'll have Socrates' *Apology*, and *King Lear*, and *Paradise Lost*, and *Pilgrim's Progress*, and *Eloise and Abelard*, and Pascal's *Pensées*, and *Gulliver's Travels*, and Wordsworth's *Intimations of Immortality*, and *Mind at the End of Its Tether* by H.G. Wells, and Huxley's *Brave New World*, and *The Screwtape Letters* by C. S. Lewis, and Mother Teresa's Nobel Prize acceptance speech. How's that for an assortment of literature! Now if I brought all these works together in a single volume and asked you, "Is it true?" then the only answer you could possibly give would be to say, "Well, yes, but the truth it holds is expressed in a great variety of ways." Believe me, the Bible is a book of far greater range and variety than the anthology I just made. It is full of truth, but not truth expressed only in literal and scientific terms, but rather truth expressed in poetry and prose and drama and parables; truth expressed in a love poem which the censors might have classified as "X-rated," "For adults only"; truth expressed by prophets, sometimes in a language of despair, sometimes in a language of hope; truth expressed in satire. In all of these ways God speaks to us through His Word. If we come to the Bible saying it is true and then proceed to narrow the truth of it to what is literally or historically true, we shall miss the richness of its treasure. So my first criticism of fundamentalists is that they say the Bible is true, but then limit the truth that the Bible is.

Secondly, fundamentalists affirm that the Bible is relevant and then proceed to trivialize its relevance. One clear instance of this is their use, or as I would say, their *abuse* of biblical prophecy.

Driving out of London recently I saw a sign outside an evangelical church. It was one of those portable illuminated signs and it said, "Armageddon, 1983, 1984, 1985?"

Armageddon is mentioned in the Book of Revelation as the last battle that will be fought at the end of the world. So the question on the sign really was, "Is the world going to end in 1983, or 1984, or

1985?" I must not have taken the question very seriously because I didn't stop for an answer. If you pass such a sign and don't stop, you don't take it very seriously either. But people who put up such signs take their predictions very seriously indeed, and they say that the relevance of the Bible is that it gives us many predictions to answer questions of that sort and tell us all that is going to happen. The Bible is relevant because it describes events and nations and characters who act in the great drama which will soon result in the end of the world. With great zeal and ingenuity, the proponents of this view of prophecy take the scriptures and apply the ancient prophecies to current events. We are told that Joel knew about atomic warfare. And Ezekiel foresaw that Ronald Reagan would be elected. And Daniel foretold that Russia would invade Afghanistan. The events of our time are all there in scripture and in prophecy. If we read them properly then we will know what will happen. This kind of preaching from prophecy is often lurid and violent and catastrophic. Some of the wilder and more confident interpreters of prophecy even put a date on it — 1983 or 1984 or 1985! And one of the most mischievous things about it is the assumption that because such disasters are prophesied in Scripture, they are inevitable. Some advocates of this view of prophecy not only predict the date of Armageddon, which they identify with a nuclear holocaust; they at times appear to relish it! How disappointing if it *didn't* happen just as they predicted!

Somebody asked me recently, "Why don't you attempt to relate prophecy to current events in this manner?" The answer is that I believe that to do so is to misunderstand the nature of prophecy, and to distort the word of God. The television evangelists who preach like this are not really preaching prophecy at all. They are preaching another kind of literature which sprang up chiefly between the Old and the New Testaments, literature of which there are only two examples in the whole Bible, the Book of Daniel and the Book of Revelation. Both are known as apocalyptic literature, whose chief characteristic is that it despairs of all things human and declares that all our affairs will be brought to an end by a catastrophic event terrible beyond imagining. The event is described in lurid colours, and with an excess of imagery and symbol, the meaning of which is not easily discerned.

But the prophets were different. They spoke primarily not of the events of a remote future time, but of their own time, interpreting them in the light of their understanding of God's nature, His righteousness, mercy and truth. They were not so much fore-tellers as forth-tellers, declaring the will of God in the events of their age. Apocalyptic literature gives up on the world, but the prophets called people to repentance, to moral uprightness, to justice and reform. The fulfillment of prophecy is not the end of the world; the fulfillment of prophecy is the incarnation, God coming in Christ to love a broken world back to sanity and wholeness. It is a distortion of the word of God to confuse the apocalyptic with the prophetic. The relevance of the Bible is not that it gives us a time-scale of events leading to the end of the world, but that it sees the events of our time and all times in the light of the judgement and mercy of God. And there is as much relevance in that as we can bear!

My third objection is that while fundamentalists declare the Bible to be the infallible word of God, they forget that God speaks through fallible men and women.

It is easy to understand why one would wish to say that the Bible is infallible, that it is in every part inerrant; because if one believes that, then one has absolute certainty in spiritual matters. That is what the fundamentalists are after. They say that when we are talking about our eternal salvation, there can be no place for doubt or uncertainty; we have got to be sure. And the way to certainty is to have an infallible book, or in the case of Roman Catholicism, an infallible Pope.

An external infallible authority, whether book or Pope, is very comforting for those who don't want to accept a measure of responsibility for their own soul. But it has an inherent weakness. You see, it isn't enough to *believe* that the Bible or the Pope is infallible. You have to be absolutely *certain* that they are. If I ask, "How do you know that the Pope is infallible," it isn't enough for you to reply, "Well, I just think he is." If I ask you how you know that the Bible is infallible, it isn't enough for you to tell me, "The Bible says it is." You must have some way of being *absolutely certain* that your infallible guide really is infallible. After all, it is certainty you are after! If you want to be absolutely certain the

Pope is infallible, there is only one way, logically, that you can be certain. You must be infallible yourself.

Now, the fundamentalists often mock Roman Catholics. They say our Roman Catholic friends are silly to think that a man could be infallible. But then they hold up their infallible book, and declare it to be an infallible guide. I ask them, "How do you know it is infallible? I don't believe it is. Most of the theologians and New Testament scholars whom I know and respect don't believe it is; so how can you be certain that it is infallible?" The answer, of course, is that they cannot know with certainty it is infallible without being infallible themselves.

The fundamentalists' basic mistake is that they misconceive the nature of inspiration. They believe that when God inspires a person He makes him into a kind of robot, an automaton. He makes him a sort of typewriter on which God taps out His message. If God did that, He would drain the chosen vessel of all the juice and flavour and richness that make him a unique person.

God doesn't work that way. There is nothing automatic about what God does with us. He doesn't work through robots; He works personally through fallible human beings. To speak through us God does not reduce us to megaphones; He elevates us to our full humanity. He doesn't make us half the person we are; He makes us twice the person we were. Inspiration is personal, not mechanical. To inspire us, God doesn't deprive us of our own spirit and insight, or even of our prejudices; instead, He heightens and enriches and quickens our minds until, at last, He speaks His own word through us. It is His word and it is our word too. It is divine, and it is human. It is authentic. But it is not infallible.

The truth is that I wouldn't want the kind of certainty which fundamentalists crave. I don't seek a faith that has more in common with mathematics than with drama and poetry. My faith is adventure and trust and doubt and conflict and tension. But, thank God, it is alive and, thank God, it is lively.

We cannot find certainty by finding an infallible Pope or an infallible book. The bible-literalist who attempts to do so is distorting the nature of scripture. We do not need such certainty. Have we not found insights in Scripture which we know to be true because they have spoken to us and found us at depths no other literature can fathom? I know that the Bible is a revelation of God because He has revealed Himself to me in it. But what it offers me is not a mathematical formula, but a gracious personal relationship of love and trust and hope.

If God has so spoken to us through His word; if through this divine and human book we have discovered who He is, and who we are, and what He wants us to do and be, need we ask for more? What reason have we to complain?

The fundamentalists say that the Bible is true and then narrow the truth which it is. They say it is relevant and then trivialize its relevance. They say it is an infallible book but forget that God speaks through fallible men and women.

One last thing. Fundamentalists declare, "The Bible says" but while they know its words, they often miss its meaning.

To quote something is not necessarily to understand it. When people repeat, "The Bible says," and when they believe they are quoting an infallible book, they are really claiming divine authority for their statement. Let's face it, once God has spoken on something there is not much point in anyone else arguing. If you want support for dogmatism how marvellous it is to have the Bible to back you up. All you need do is to say "The Bible says" and the matter is settled.

Well, I think the Bible *says*. Don't you? But I think the Bible says all sorts of things. First, it says all kinds of things that have no authority for you and me. The Bible says that we ought not to eat pork. Do you? The Bible says that we ought to observe the Sabbath which is the seventh day, the last day of the week. How many of you observe that? If you did you would go to church on Saturdays. The Bible says that blasphemers and adulterers should be stoned to death. Is that what you believe? And so it goes on, "The Bible says!" but the Bible says a great many things which have no hold on Christian people. We simply do not recognize them as authoritative for us.

Second, note that when people say "The Bible says" they are affirming that all parts of the Bible are equally inspired. So they can choose a text from anywhere, Leviticus, Proverbs, St. John's Gospel; each bit has the same absolute authority. I believe that to be pernicious nonsense. Most of the Old Testament does not have the power or authority for me which the New Testament has. I judge what it says in the light of and by the spirit of Christ. The most authoritative thing in Scripture is the grace and truth of our Lord, and everything else comes under His judgement.

James M. Barrie once said that if he took his mother's Bible and set it on a table it would open itself at the 14th Chapter of John's Gospel. That was the authoritative Scripture for her. It nourished her more than any other part. Henry Drummond used to say that he lived in the 13th Chapter of the First Letter to the Corinthians, that great hymn of love. Drummond promised anyone who would read that chapter every day that it would transform their life. That was the heart of the Scriptures for him. You and I have favourite parts of Scripture, parts that speak to us to rebuke and nourish us. Said one great Bible reader, "This book has wrestled with me; the book has smitten me; the book has comforted me; the book has smiled on me; the book has frowned on me; the book has clasped my hand; the book weeps with me and sings with me; it whispers to me and it preaches to me; it maps my way, and holds up all my goings."

There are some bits of the Bible which have never spoken to me at all. Some day perhaps they will. But they have not yet. So don't tell me that every text of Scripture is as good as every other text; I do not believe that the Book of Leviticus is as significant for a Christian as St. John's Gospel. I will not accept that the Book of Numbers has the authority for us that the Sermon on the Mount has. To say so is to talk nonsense. Yes, "The Bible says," but each part of the Bible is not equally authoritative.

Also, notice this. When you say "The Bible says" you ignore the fact that the Bible is all the time carrying on a debate within itself. There is not one view in the Bible. There are many views.

The psalmist says that if we trust God, He will reward us with long life and health and ease and plenty. The Book of Job declares that to be nonsense and contends for a deeper view of God's providence. Job demands of God an explanation of the inequities of life and charges that the psalmist's words do not square with human experience. Some scriptures teach "an eye for an eye and a tooth for a tooth," but it was our Lord who said we should love our enemies and do good to them that hate us. It is not enough just to say "The Bible says," because the Bible carries on a debate with itself from beginning to end. It contends with itself to find something better to say!

The reason this is so is that the Bible is a progressive revelation. It doesn't end where it started. It starts with a local God who was interested only in one nation and was restricted to their territory. It ends with a God who encompasses all the world in His love so that, like invited guests at a wedding feast, people come from north and south and east and west and take their place in the Father's kingdom. The Bible begins with a warrior God who could tell Joshua to go into the cities of the plain and massacre everyone who was there including the women, the children, and even the animals. It ends with Christ saying, "Let the children come to me for of such is the Kingdom of God," and assuring those who heard Him that whether they were Jew or gentile, the very hairs of their heads were numbered.

We pray that God will lead us by His spirit into truth, but the truth of God is not a written word, but a Living Word. Christ is Lord, even of the scriptures. Anything that I read in the Bible must be in harmony with His spirit, His love, His teaching. Otherwise, it has no authority for me. I hold to Him and to the rest I am uncommitted.

There is inspiration and power and revelation and authority in the Bible because if we will listen to it and if we will hear it, it will lead us to Him in whom is all the fullness of God. The Bible is, as Martin Luther said, the cradle in which our Lord Christ is laid. What greater claim would one wish to make for it than that?

THREE VERDICTS ON LIFE

"The light shines on in the dark, and the darkness has never quenched it."

St. John 1:5

My topic is "Three Views of Life" or, better still, "Three Verdicts on Life." Have you ever considered your basic attitude towards life? Our basic attitude to something is our verdict on it, our decision about it. But there is a sense in which it is not life that is on trial, we are! Stephen Crane put it nicely in a poem called *The Man*:

A Man said to the universe,
"Sir, I exist!"
"However," replied the universe,
"The fact has not created in me
A sense of obligation."

When we declare our own verdict, it is not only a judgement on life but on ourselves, for it reveals our expectation, our disposition, our character; whether we are cynical or trustful, captured by despair or prisoners of hope, part of the world's problem or part of its solution. Let me suggest to you three verdicts on life, and ask you to decide which one is yours; which verdict comes closest to how you judge life and its meaning.

The first verdict is that life is good enough to be true. In other words, life really does meet and satisfy one's expectations.

Those who return this verdict expect life to be good and are not disappointed. They conclude, from the evidence, that it *is* good. It is good enough to be true, and they embrace it with joy.

This verdict on life is both old and new. It is expressed both in religious and secular thought. It is expressed in religious terms by those Christians who believe that it is God's responsibility to ensure the goodness of life by supplying our wants, ministering to our comfort, rewarding the good and punishing the wicked. In such a world life fulfills all our expectations. It is just, wisely governed by a benevolent providence, and once you know the rules you can accommodate yourself to them very nicely and be at peace with things. At times the Psalmist came very close to this view of life, and so did the conventionally religious friends of Job, those who came to try and comfort him when he thought that God had let him down. They told Job that the real trouble was with him, not with life, which was good enough to be true.

Sometimes this verdict is expressed in philosophical terms. Leibniz, for example, worked out a meticulous philosophy designed to show that everything is for the best in this best of all possible worlds. And Alexander Pope, in his *Essay on Man*, very powerfully expressed the same view, "Whatever is, is right." There was a place for everything and everything was in its place, and that meant not just things, but people as well.

The view that life is good enough to be true was given a modern twist by those nineteenth-century progressive thinkers who took the idea of evolution from biology, where it properly belonged, and applied it to everything. Herbert Spencer said we had achieved not just a theory of evolutionary progress, but the reality of inevitable progress. We were marching onwards and upwards into a glorious future unfolding for us.

It is hard for us today to imagine the feeling of confidence which this idea of inevitable progress brought to people. It gave them a sense of destiny, not only about their lives, but about life itself. Not only was nature perfectible, but natural selection and evolution were engines remorselessly driving life to perfection. Every day in every way, we were getting better and better. An American president confidently predicted that in a few years poverty would be abolished, medicine would heal all diseases and finally conquer death itself. Education would dispel ignorance. The Social Sciences would put right all the thorny social problems. Utopia was not a crazy dream, it was just around the corner. The difficult we could do at once; the impossible would take only a little longer.

Any lingering doubts were dispelled by the great Russian experiment, so beloved of the intelligensia of the Western world. They went to Russia to see for themselves and came back and pronounced it good. "I have seen the future, and it works" proclaimed Lincoln Steffens. The great Soviet experiment was going to usher in the Kingdom of heaven on earth with Josef Stalin as its patron saint.

Of course, there was no need for God in such Utopias. We had outgrown religious dogma. Mankind had come of age. Brave new world! Men like gods! Sin was nothing but an "evolutionary overhang!"

What a monstrous bloody fraud it was! Tens of millions of innocent Russian peasants, according to Alexander Solzhenitsyn, killed either by firing squad or by forced labour in the Gulag Archipelago. Stalin demonstrated once again that a man may smile and smile and be a villain.

The trouble was, you see, that reality, reality in the shape of people and events, just kept breaking in. Malcolm Muggeridge once said that the trouble with Utopias is that they are likely to come to pass and then their threadbare pretentions are obvious for all to see. When a Utopia ceases to be a dream and becomes a reality, we see it for what it really is.

Centuries ago, reality broke in on the complacent, ordered world of Job. For years his life had been good enough to be true, fulfilling all his expectations, realizing all his hopes. And then, suddenly, everything changed. He discovered the perverseness of life, that it is not always just, that the good do not always flourish nor the wicked always perish. When that happened, Job raged against life and against God. He shook his fist in the face of the Almighty and demanded answers. Job is every one of us who by pain and sorrow has discovered that ours is not a perfect existence, and that life is not always good enough to be true.

Reality broke in on Voltaire. A great earthquake hit Lisbon in 1755; not only an earthquake, but a fire and a tidal wave that swept through the city and killed thousands of people. But Lisbon was no more wicked than any other city. And there were more people killed in the churches than in the brothels. How do you square that with this idea of a perfect world? Voltaire could not, and so he wrote

Candide, that witty play which satirizes the whole idea of the perfectibility of human nature.

This generation does not need to go back to the great fire of Lisbon. We have lived through a depression, two world wars, and the horrors of the concentration camps in Germany and in Russia which have demonstrated for us the depravity of human nature. Before that we thought virtue was easy, and confidently and cheerfully exhorted everybody to be brotherly and kind and loving and good. Then, suddenly, we had Belsen and Buchenwald and Dachau; and all the easy assumptions were gone. Life good enough to be true? It is too easy a verdict for a child of this century!

Then came our disillusionment with science. Slowly we came to realize that while evolution may be a useful theory in biology it does not explain man or his nature. As one of our modern poets tells us, "We have impetus but not progress. We have cleverness but not wisdom."

So Will Durant wrote a letter to his "famous contemporaries" — and they are your contemporaries and mine — and in despair he asked them, "What is the meaning of human life? Thought seems to have destroyed itself. Knowledge has brought us only disillusionment. Truth has not made us glad; why did we hurry to find it? It has taken from us every reason for existence except the moment's pleasure and tomorrow's trivial hope. And behind it all, there is the bomb." One of our poets wrote a poem; she called it, *Epitaph For the Race of Man.* We live in what one writer called, "The Morning after Optimism."

So there is one attitude to life. Life is good enough to be true. What do you think of it?

That brings me to a second verdict on life. It is that life is too good to be true. And because it is too good to be true, you can't trust it. You must always be suspicious. It looks good, but don't be deceived, because lurking just beneath the surface is a perverse malevolence that is out to get us. So be suspicious of your happiness because when you are happiest, that is when fate puts the knife in, and twists it. Oblivious to their fate the victims play. As Gloucester declares in *King Lear,*

> "As flies to wanton boys, are we to the Gods; They kill us for their sport."

So don't trust life! It's too good to be true! The appropriate attitude is suspicion and cynicism.

I blush to say it, but the Irish are about the worst offenders in this attitude, and especially those whose occupation puts them at the mercy of forces they cannot control — the weather, for example. You can never get an Irish farmer to say it's a great day. He is afraid that if he says it's a good day today, it will be a bad day tomorrow. Because something is out to get him, he mustn't tempt fate. Such people can become terribly superstitious. At Queen's University in Belfast there was a fairy thorn tree. It cast its shade over the Senate Room. When the university wanted it cut down they could not find anyone to do it. They were all afraid that if they did, they'd pay for it. The wee folk would get them. So the university had to change the plans, and for all I know the fairy tree is still standing. This happened at Queen's University in Belfast where the Senate Room is surrounded by six scientific departments!

Thank God we are not like that, or maybe we are. Do you ever hesitate to say to your wife, "The car is running well," or, "I haven't had a cold all winter?" We're almost afraid to say such things. We suspect that there is a kind of perverseness about life so that we are afraid to be happy. If we are happy something will come along to put a blight on our happiness. There will be weeping for all our laughter. Some say life is too good to be true, so don't trust it!

Why are we like this? Perhaps for some it goes back to childhood. Some of us had loved ones in our childhood who constantly reassured us. By their love and confidence and care and faithfulness they enabled us to feel that whatever went wrong, everything would be all right. It's easy for some of us to have a trustful attitude to life and to God and to people because that is the way we were brought up. All our lives we have been surrounded by people who loved us and whom we could trust.

For others it is not so easy. A girl in her late teens once came to see me in Toronto. As far as I could discover, she had never had a trustful relationship with anyone in her life. She had no reason to trust anybody. As soon as she was old enough to understand, her parents informed her that her coming into the world was an accident. They hadn't planned her. They didn't want her. They gave her a nickname and it stuck, even with her friends. Do you know what they called her? Homely! To call your own child, or any child that! When she came to see me, she was not really trusting me; she was just a tiny bit hopeful because I had been able to help her brother who was in prison. She had approached other people and they had all tried to use her; they wanted to sleep with her, or to exploit her in some way; and so she came to me not really believing that she could have confidence in me or anybody or anything. It is a heavy responsibility to be the slender thread of trust for somebody. When you meet someone like that young girl, how can you say, "Trust God!" or, "Trust life!" Their whole experience of living has taught them to be suspicious. They do not know what it means to trust God because they have never had the experience of trusting anyone worthy of their confidence.

Sometimes the wrong kind of religious faith can create that sense of distrust. A good part of the religion in which some of us grew up really believed, regardless of what it *said,* that God is against us. We were told that He loved us, but how many of us ever really believed that He liked us? He was constantly there, out on the fringes, and we were never quite sure what He was going to do. You couldn't count on Him. He couldn't be trusted. Life was splendid as long as it went along happily, but when sorrow or grief or pain came then the old cynicism about God reasserted itself. The good times were not to be trusted, for He was merely having sport with us. We knew it all the time. He didn't deceive us for a minute. The evil was what we really expected. Our afflictions showed us what God was really like. Life was too good to be true.

Thomas Hardy's novels exemplify this attitude. We come to expect the cruel twist of fate, and know that the gods are playing a game with men's lives. It is so easy to fall into the belief that life is out to get us! There are so many instances that seem to bear this theory out. Here is a husband and wife who worked hard all their lives. The mortgage is paid off now and the children are educated. They are looking forward to retirement. They intend to travel together, to do all the things that formerly they didn't have the time or the money to do. Life looks wonderful. Then, just a couple of months after retirement, he dies from a heart attack. It is so cruel! It seems that life set them up so that in the end it could knock them down. I think of C. S. Lewis who made a promise during the war that he would look after a friend's mother. And so he did. For thirty years he looked after her, and a bitter, selfish woman she was. And then, after thirty years, she died. With the prospect of a few good years left, Lewis met Joy Davidman and they fell in love and they married. What unexpected bliss for him! But it was to prove brief, for they discovered that Joy had cancer. She became weak; but then the disease went into remission and their hopes rose again. Then the cancer returned more virulent than ever, and she died. Not long after, he died too. When you and I look at this it seems to us that life made them great promises and then cruelly broke them. It gave a gift and then snatched it back. It offered them wine and then dashed the cup from their lips just as they went to drink. How easy it is to believe that life is too good to be true!

People who have had a family pet run over know the feeling. "We won't get another one. It's too painful," they say. The young man whose love has been spurned knows the feeling. "I'll never give my heart away again," he says bitterly. How can we trust life? How can we trust God? Once bitten, twice shy! It was Reinhold Niebuhr who declared that under our modern smiles run deep rivers of cynicism and despair. We believe that life is too good to be true.

Is that you? If so, you have distinguished company. It was Bertrand Russell who, in one of the most beautiful passages he ever wrote, advised people to build their lives on a foundation of unshakeable despair, assuming, I suppose, that if you never expect anything you'll never be disappointed.

I cannot accept that, for it is impossible to do it. You cannot sensibly talk about building on foundations of despair. If you talk of building then it means you are not despairing. To be consistent, Russell must despair of building on despair. But even he can't manage that! So, too, when we attempt to be thoroughgoing cynics, we find faith and hope and love breaking through to reassert themselves. Ignazio Silone once said that if the whole world were plastered over with concrete, somewhere, sometime, a tiny crack would appear and, through that crack, a rose would bloom.

So there are those who say that life is good enough to be true; the cosmic optimists, the wishful thinkers. And there are those who say life is too good to be true; the cynics, the disillusioned.

But there is another view, another verdict. It says that life is not good enough to be true.

Some years ago, Sir Oliver Lodge sat down to write a new catechism. The first question was, "What are you?" The second question was — and this was a stroke of purest genius — "What then does the fall of man mean?" Think about those two questions. What are you? What then does the fall of man mean?

G. K. Chesterton came to these two questions in his whimsical, brilliant way. The first one, "What are you?" he answered, "God knows!" Then the second one, "What then does the fall of man mean?" Chesterton answered, "It means that whatever I am, I am not myself!"

Isn't that marvellous? What are you? God knows! What then does the fall of man mean? It means that whatever I am, I am not myself. You see, the real truth about Chesterton and about me and you is that we are better than what we are. We are not ourselves. We are not good enough to be true. The truth of us is better than anything we have yet realized.

Do you not see the truth of this when you examine yourself? Don't you know that there is something that you have missed? Are you not haunted by a destiny unrealized? Are there not immortal longings in you which refute all that is sordid and mean in your life? This is what Chesterton meant. "Whatever I am, I am not myself." I have not realized what I was created to be.

This is exactly the way in which Jesus looked at life and at people. He looked at the world and said, "It isn't good enough to be true, and because it isn't good enough to be true God has sent me to make it as good as He intended it to be." That is why Jesus could be angry. A Stoic never gets angry, he remains stoical and learns to accept things as they are. How can you be angry in the best of all possible worlds? But Jesus got angry! Why? Because the religion of the Temple wasn't good enough to be true. Because the hypocrisy of the Pharisees was not worthy of them. He had double vision; He saw them both as they were and as they might be. Cynics do not weep. Jesus wept! He wept over a world that was not as good as God meant it to be. Everywhere He looked He saw the divine intention frustrated. He wept over Jerusalem which did not know its time of visitation and failed to recognize God's moment when it came. And under the anger and the tears was God's unwearied love, reconciling the world to Himself, seeking to make it what He wanted it to be. There is an old Hebridean prayer which is inexpressibly poignant. It says, "Take me often from the tumult of things into Thy presence. There show me what I am and what Thou hast purposed me to be. Then hide me from Thy tears."

Now there is an understanding of sin for you! Not just the transgression of a commandment, but the disappointment of a loving purpose. Not just the breaking of a divine law, but the breaking of a divine heart and the frustrating of all that Eternal Love could accomplish in and through us. Jesus believed that life was not good enough to be true. Why? Because He believed that God is good, that He is better than we have ever thought or imagined. The message of the Gospel is simply that God is closer to us than we have ever known; more loving, more willing to help us than we are either to ask or to receive. And that what He intends for us is great beyond our imagining. Our Lord declared that God is therefore worthy of our trust, and He put Himself behind His words and lived and died trusting Him.

Do you believe Him? In the end, that is the question. It is the only question of faith. Do you believe Him? Was He the dreamer or the only one awake? Who is upside down, Jesus or us? Who is the sane one and who is mad? That is the question you must ponder. Make up your mind about that.

I think of the French writer who in 1908 wrote a book entitled, *The Insanity of Jesus*. If that writer is correct, then I for one want that kind of insanity. This world needs that kind of madness. Said Malcolm Muggeridge, "If there is no light in Him, then there is no light." I would much rather trust His certainties than my doubts.

If you believe Him, there is something more. Another step to take. It is to become the instrument of His goodness. Because life isn't good enough to be true we hear a call to serve that goodness which life may yet be. Socrates knew that. Speaking of his ideal city he says, "It matters not if this ideal city has ever been, or in fact will ever be, *for he who has seen it will live in the manner of the city*."

Once upon a time we thought we could hold the light so high that we could banish the darkness. It would be the best of all possible worlds. But we couldn't do it.

Then we became cynical and believed the darkness to be so deep and impenetrable that it would extinguish our light. But that did not happen either. The darkness has not been able to quench it.

So where do Christians stand now? We have learned that we are not able to banish the darkness. Neither are we driven to despair, content to "sit in darkness and the shadow of death," afraid that the darkness will overwhelm us. We are called to reflect His light, and so shine in the darkness. And the promise is that His light will shine, and the darkness will never be able to put it out.

> This little light of mine,
> I'm going to let it shine.
> Let it shine!
> Let it shine!
> Let it shine!

PREVENIENT GRACE

"From first to last this has been the work of God."

2 Corinthians 5:18

I want to talk to you about "Prevenient Grace." Some of you are puzzled by the title, and wonder what it means. What is *Prevenient* Grace, or Preventing Grace, a term which is even better because it is biblical?

I can best answer your question by telling you a story first told by Dr. Leslie Weatherhead. It is about Hugh Redwood, a celebrated lay preacher in England. He was often invited, not only to preach in churches, but to address large public meetings. Thousands of people came to hear him.

At one period in his life, Hugh Redwood passed through a difficult time. He had some very hard decisions to make, and wasn't sure what he should do. He asked God for guidance, but as sometimes happens, it seemed that no guidance was given. The heavens were silent. One evening he went to have dinner with some friends before going on to address a large public meeting of several thousand people. When the meal was over his hostess said to him, "Hugh, don't wait around for the small talk; go upstairs to the study. There is a fire burning. Put your feet up and relax for a little while." Redwood was glad of a little peace and quiet, so that is what he did. He found, as promised, that there was a cheery fire in the grate. He sat down on an easy chair and noticed that on the table beside the chair was a Bible. He picked it up and discovered that it was open at Psalm 59. He began to read, and when he came to Verse 10 he found the words, "The God of my mercy shall prevent me."

The word "prevent" is a word that has changed its meaning. Nowadays if we prevent somebody it means that we stop them from doing something. But when the King James Version of the Bible was produced the word "prevent" meant "to go before." To prevent someone was to go before them. The text really meant, "The God of my mercy shall go before me." But somebody else had written another translation in the margin, and it found its way into Hugh Redwood's mind with such power that he never forgot it. The anonymous hand had written, "My God, in His loving kindness, shall meet me at every corner." For Hugh Redwood that text was light in a dark place. The hard decisions were made, and they proved to be wise ones. He went on to accomplish great things and to live a useful and fulfilled life.

Now that's prevenient grace! Do you know what it says to us? It tells us that God is not only behind us in forgiveness and with us as a loving, strengthening Presence; He is also out in front of us beckoning us into a future that is already filled with His goodness. In His loving kindness He meets us at every corner.

When I was at theological college, we had a Scottish professor who used to say, "Magnify your certainties!" The trouble with us is that we magnify our *un*certainties. When we talk about the future we say that we don't know what a day will bring forth. And because we cannot see the future, we "guess and fear," as Robert Burns put it. We guess and fear when we ought to be magnifying our certainties. One of our certainties is that the future into which we journey is already filled with God. It is not empty. It is not totally mysterious. If we are Christians we believe that it is filled with a gracious Presence who beckons to us, and for our guesses and fears offers confidence and hope.

This can make an enormous difference to your life. Some people think that their life is like a line drawn on a piece of paper. They draw the horizontal line which represents their pilgrimage, and then they draw other vertical lines across the horizontal line and say, "This is where God came in!" What they say is true, but it is not the whole truth, and it is not the best truth. You see, if the story of our life is like a line drawn on a sheet of paper, then God is not another intersecting line, but the page on which the line is drawn! He encompasses us at every point. There is no place at which His loving action does not touch our life. Dame Julian of Norwich expressed it perfectly when she wrote, "We are all in Him enclosed." That is, we are wrapped round by goodness and love. Not only forgiven for what is past and strengthened in the present, but drawn into a future that is filled with divine mercy.

Think, for a moment, of the difference that truth could make if you were to say to yourself whenever you find yourself in distressing circumstances, when you are anxious, when your heart is terrified at what tomorrow will bring, "My God, in His loving kindness, shall meet me at every corner." Wouldn't that be enormously strengthening and reassuring? Every life has its corners. We can't see around them and because we don't know what is waiting for us we are apprehensive. We are not sure what demand will be made upon our wisdom, or understanding, or courage, or fortitude, or sensitivity. And so we are afraid.

But suppose we were to say, and to keep on saying to ourselves, "God is already there! Before I enter this experience of anxiety or weakness, God is already present strengthening me for it and meeting me in it." Wouldn't that affirmation strengthen our confidence and renew our courage?

Every life has its corners. Think of some of them! I remember as though it were yesterday my first day at school. Do you remember yours? You found yourself in a strange place, entrusted to people you did not know. Do you remember the day you started university? You were pretty clever in high school, but in high school you were a big fish in a small pond. Now in university you were a small fish in a big pond. And you didn't know how you would measure up to the fiercer competition, and you were apprehensive.

Do you remember when you left home and took your first job? You were astonished that anybody would give you a job to begin with, and you hardly knew what you were going to do with it now that you had it. What if you failed? That was menacing, wasn't it?

Do you remember when you got married? We think it a happy thing to plan a wedding, and of course it is. But very often brides and grooms will say to me, "I am really afraid. I am not sure that it will work." They know how many marriages end in divorce, and wonder if they'll be able to make and keep each other happy.

Do you remember when you retired? Better still, do you remember when your husband retired? It meant you were going to have him around the house all day. That was menacing, wasn't it?

You didn't know what you were going to do with the old boy. And he didn't know what he was going to do with himself. He had been a man of authority, and people had looked up to him, and he had an office to go to. Now that was all over, and the change was frightening.

And, of course, there is that corner which we all must turn because we are mortal. We go into "the undiscovered country from whose bourne no traveller returns." And that is the last menacing thing. It is what Heidegger called, "the iron ring around existence," the last horizon, the final mystery. And the thought of death can terrify us.

Think, then, of the difference it makes when we know that in all of these threatening circumstances there is a mercy that goes before us to meet us at every corner. There is a young fellow in my congregation in London who is a fine hockey player. He was playing hockey one evening and was hit in the eye by the puck. He was brought to University Hospital and for a little while he didn't know how badly his eye had been injured. He said, "You know, Dr. Boyd, as I went up to the hospital I just kept saying to myself, 'My God, in His loving kindness, shall meet me at every corner.'"

One day I visited a woman from a rural community who had been brought to hospital in the city. She was terminally ill, and she knew it. She said, "As they were wheeling me along the corridors into one room after another to perform all those tests which leave you with little comfort and no dignity, I said to myself, as I turned this corner and that, 'My God, in His loving kindness, shall meet me at every corner.'"

I don't know what your particular predicament is; I don't know whether you are worried about your health, or your children, or your future, or your marriage, or your job. But I do know that an essential part of our faith is to believe that we are not alone in our trouble, and that the future is not hopeless. In His loving kindness, God is already there.

Now that is the first thing. I wanted to tell you what a difference it would make to every part of your life if you really believed that, "My God, in His loving kindness, shall meet me at every corner."

Here is the second thing. I want to show you that once you grasp the truth of preventing or prevenient grace, and have a sense

Lost
emotionally
physically
spiritually

of God always acting first, then no part of your understanding of Him will remain untouched. And it seems to me that this, more than anything else, is the message that the church needs to hear because the Christian church in many ways has become a graceless church. We have lost the reality and the wonder of God's grace.

This is an open-ended sermon. I am going to toss out five or six instances of how our understanding of God is enhanced by the truth that grace is prevenient. I hope that you won't leave it there. Go on thinking about it. Find other examples in your own experience, other insights into your understanding of God which will be deepened when you believe that God always acts first.

For example, notice what the truth of prevenient grace does to our idea of finding God. We sometimes talk as though we spent all our time searching for God while He spent most of His time trying to avoid us. We pursue one who is reluctant to be found. We cry out with Job, "Oh that I knew where I might find Him!"

How can I find God? That is like a bird asking, "How can I find the air?" or a fish asking, "How can I find the ocean?" We couldn't even think of finding God if He had not already found us! Do we not know that "it is in Him that we live and move and have our being?" It was Blaise Pascal who expressed the truth of this perfectly by telling us that we could not seek God if He had not already found us! We seek Him and the very power of our search is God's life in us. We pursue Him with our heart and the very motion of our heart is the action of His grace. We long for Him with our spirit, and what is our spirit but the candle of the Lord? We look for Him with our mind, and He is the light of the mind that seeks Him. C. S. Lewis said that when people talk about their search for God it is like the mouse speaking of his search for the cat.

Religion at its best has always known this. It has known that the very best we can offer to God is but our response to His loving initiative. In other words, all true religion has discovered that God's grace is prevenient.

I sought the Lord, and afterward I knew
He moved my soul to seek Him, seeking me;
It was not I that found, O Saviour true —
No, I was found of Thee.

I find, I walk, I love, but O the whole
Of Love is but my answer, Lord, to Thee;
For Thou wast long beforehand with my soul,
Always Thou lovedst me.

Prevenient grace! It reminds us that all our searching for God is a sign that He has already found us.

Here is another thing. Notice how the experience of prevenient grace enhances our understanding of repentance. When I turn on the television evangelists or listen to preachers on radio, my objection to most of them is not that they are too evangelical but that they are not evangelical enough. Do you know what they say? They say that if we repent God will forgive us. And they tell us that that is the gospel. That isn't the gospel! Do you think it is? If you think it is then you need to adjust your thinking.

"If you repent God will forgive you" they say, but the whole trick is repenting. How do you do it? Of *course* if you repent God will forgive you. But how do you repent? The truth is that you can't repent without God's help. Your repentance is itself God's gracious work. You couldn't repent if He did not enable you to do so. It is not true to say that we repent and then God forgives us. He is already at work, graciously bringing us to repentance. For this reason it is not true to say that God forgives us because we repent. It *is* true to say that we repent because God has forgiven us. God's forgiveness of us in His gracious initiative reaching out to us and enabling us to repent! You see, the initiative is His. His grace stretches out to us when we don't know how to repent. John Donne put it splendidly, "Here on this lowly ground, teach me how to repent; for that's as good as if Thou hadst sealed my pardon with Thy blood."

Not long after we came to a church in Sarnia, somebody asked us, "Have you been to Brigden Fair?" Brigden is a small town not far from Sarnia, well-known for the excellence of its Fall Fair. Well, we hadn't been to Brigden Fair, so off we went. Our daughter Jennifer was just a tiny little girl at the time, and we lost her at Brigden Fair. We blinked our eyes and she was gone. We started to look for her, sick with fright. Have you ever read about the taste of fear? And you thought it was a mere figure of speech, didn't you? Let me tell you that it is literally true. There is a taste of fear, and I

tasted it that day. I could imagine that tiny little morsel of humanity
lost among all the people and the roundabouts and the animals. I
could imagine her being absolutely terrified at not being able to find
us. It took us about fifteen minutes to find her. We discovered her
wandering nonchalantly about the place, having the time of her life,
enjoying every moment of it. You see, the truth is that Jennifer
didn't know she was lost until we found her.

You may think the gospel message is that if you are lost and
return to God you will be reconciled and forgiven. But the gospel is
better than that. The gospel is that He comes to seek and to save us
before we know we are lost. That's prevenient grace! Said P.T.
Forsythe, a great theologian, "Don't tell people how they ought to
feel about Christ. Preach a Christ who will make them feel how
they ought to feel."

Let me tell you another way in which prevenient grace deepens
our understanding of the Faith. This one has to do with our forgiveness of other people. I remember having a church in which a
woman came to see me and told me, "It's a terrible thing, but when
I come to church I feel shut out; closed out by God. You see, when I
was a tiny little girl my father did things to me that I can't forgive. I
have been trying all my life and I can't find it in me to forgive him.
And when I come to church, I hear the words of Scripture and they
seem to say that if I don't forgive my father, God won't forgive me;
that we are forgiven only if we are willing to forgive. But I cannot
forgive. This makes me think that God has closed me out, that I am
beyond the reach of His mercy. What am I to do?" Her distress was
very great.

What would you have said to her? I answered her by saying,
"What if God really loves you, and loves you not because of
anything you have done or left undone, but loves you first?" I said
to her, "Suppose that He isn't standing over against you, making a
demand, issuing an ultimatum by saying, 'If you don't forgive him, I
won't forgive you.' What if God is already on your side, helping
you to do what you cannot do in your own strength? What if He
doesn't merely ask that you forgive, but *enables* you to forgive?"
The woman went home to think about what I had said, and a few
weeks later we met together in the empty church and she renewed
her vows of church membership. Do you know what she had

discovered? She had discovered the reality and wonder of prevenient grace. In the strength of that grace she had come to forgive her father. It is by being forgiven that we are enabled to forgive. Said St. Augustine, "Demand what thou wilt, but first, give me what Thou dost demand!" That is exactly what God does, and we call that loving initiative prevenient grace.

Notice how the same idea will illumine our understanding of Christian assurance. The doctrine of Christian assurance is very precious to me because I was brought up a Methodist, and one of the cardinal doctrines of Methodism is that you not only may be saved, but may have the assurance that you are saved. But while the assurance of salvation is a Methodist doctrine, it made me feel very uncomfortable. What bothered me was that so many of the people who were sure of their salvation were insufferable. They were not only sure, they were cocksure. They were arrogant. They used their assurance of salvation to make other Christians who were less sure feel inferior.

But it's not enough simply to complain about them. We ought to discover *why* they offend us. Is it just their presumptuousness? Is it their condescension? Is it their arrogance? It is all of these things, but that isn't the heart of their offensiveness. I think I know what it is that disturbs me about them. It is that they regard Christian assurance as something which they themselves have accomplished. They wave it like a flag, wear it like a medal. And that isn't Christian assurance at all. Christian assurance isn't anything we have accomplished or achieved, it is something which God has done. It is His work, not ours.

Suppose you were to ask how I know that my wife loves me. I could go two ways on that. I could say, for example, "How could she help it?" And if I were to say that, you would do one of two things; you would either groan and say, "Well, how insufferable can you get!" or you would have a good chuckle. Now that's one way of answering the question, but there is another way. Suppose I were to say to you, "Well, I know my wife loves me because in her great kindness she constantly reassures me of her love." Now, you see, that's different, isn't it? Because that assurance is not in me, it's in her. It is not something of which I can boast, it is something for which I am thankful. It is not something I have accomplished, but something which she has bestowed. It doesn't lead to arrogance but to humility. It is not anything I have achieved, but something I have received.

Christian assurance is like that. It is not something we possess as though we had done it ourselves. It is something which God graciously does for us. And that's the wonder of it. Our assurance is but a response to His gracious initiative who in His great kindness constantly reassures us of His love.

Just one thing more. Notice how prevenient grace sheds light on our understanding of our own good works. Sometimes we think that we have a claim on God because we are good. The New Testament reveals this quite clearly. Do you remember the Pharisee who strutted in the Divine presence having made a kind of inventory of his goodness, and boasted of his virtue? What he did not realize is that even our goodness is God's work in us. It's not something we may use to establish a claim on Him; it is something which He has accomplished in us.

Let me tell you another story about the Jennifer we lost at Brigden Fair. Not long after we arrived in Sarnia, we planted three thousand tulip bulbs. It was a small garden or we would have planted more. And the next spring, one of them came up. And one day Jennifer went into the garden and plucked this tulip. She brought it in and gave it to her mother as a gift. Now that was pretty silly, wasn't it? It was her mother's tulip all the time. My wife had planted it, and looked after it. It was hers. It wasn't Jennifer's to give to her. And yet she received Jennifer's gift with smiling face, and thanked her for it.

It is like that with God. We come to Him bringing our goodness and presenting it to Him as a gift, when all the time it is His work, who is the Fountain of all goodness. And He is so gracious that He is honoured by our gift, and receives it lovingly. That is the greatness of God's reticence and humility. He accomplishes everything, and yet allows us to think that the work is all ours! We need to remind ourselves often that,

> Every virtue we possess;
> And every conquest won;
> And every thought of holiness;
> Is His alone.

I hope I have said enough about prevenient grace to enable you to go on thinking about it, and to find further instances of it in your own experience. You see, it's really very simple. It just means that before God makes any demand of us He enables us to give Him what He demands. He enables us to do what He requires of us. And that means we are never without His help. We are never rejected. We are never forsaken. We are never alone.

Let me tell you just one more story. It is about Dr. Campbell Morgan who was a great preacher in England some years ago. One day he went to visit a member of his church, only to learn that she was to be evicted from her house because she couldn't pay the rent. That was on Saturday afternoon, so on Sunday Campbell Morgan told his congregation that he wanted enough money from them to pay the woman's rent. They gave it to him. First thing on Monday morning he went to the woman's house with the money. He could hardly wait to tell her the good news. He hammered on the door, but there was no answer. What a disappointment! He knocked again, but no one answered, and he went sadly away. Some time later he discovered that the woman had been at home all the time. She had been afraid to answer the door, for she thought it was the landlord who had come for the rent, and all the time it was her minister bringing her the money she needed.

That is like our misunderstanding of God. We think he comes making a demand when what He really does is bring us a gift.

The sermon is over, and yet I can't quite leave it there. You see, it's not enough for me to say to you, "If you believe what I have told you it will make a difference to your life." I must say something more if I am to be true to my message. I must say to you that in this very instant, in this moment while you are listening to my voice, God is graciously present enabling you to believe and to trust His goodness. And that's prevenient grace! The moment you believe it and receive it your religion ceases to be a burden. Rather, it becomes the kind of burden wings are to a bird, and sails are to a ship.

HAPPY AT HOME

Psalm 68:6

Statistics Canada reports that nearly half of this year's marriages will end in divorce. Think of that! All those nervous grooms, all those radiant brides, standing side by side making their promises, feeling inseparable; yet almost half will some day stand alone in a lawyer's office or a divorce court, their hopes and expectations and plans and dreams all behind them, shattered.

Even more shocking than statistics are those occasions when statistics become flesh and blood and the sadness of divorce is brought home to us personally. We suddenly discover that couples we have known and respected and loved, couples we have thought of for years as couples, have separated. We don't think of figures or charts; we think of Mary and John, and Fred and Margaret, people who have been our friends and our neighbours. We think of them together. We love them both. And then suddenly we discover that while we love them both, they no longer love each other.

I don't know how this affects you, but when it happens to me I experience many of the emotions I feel when I hear that someone I know has died. There is the same sense of shock and the same sense of personal loss. Friends and acquaintances who have been part of the fabric of our life suddenly are no longer together. It is like a death.

I saw a recent newspaper report of a woman who was married to a lawyer and he was killed in a motor accident. The court limited the amount of compensation she received by the number of years the judge estimated they would have stayed married. When the couple pledged their vows it was "till death do us part" and now, in a courtroom, a judge measured out the life expectancy of their

83

marriage as a draper measures out cloth. The judge said it was silly to ignore the statistics and to think they were going to be together for the rest of their lives. So he calculated compensation on the number of years that statistics reveal they were likely to stay married to each other. Those words, so full of promise and of hope, "till death do us part," counted for nothing. Now that's how it is for many people, and when you add in the number of separations, formal and informal, and the number of parents who stay together for the sake of the children, this all adds up to a great deal of human misery.

We cannot ignore it. We see it all around us, in our neighbourhood, at work, in our congregation. It is part of our life now. The anthropologist, Margaret Mead, recently revealed that she was shocked to discover how many couples setting out on marriage today no longer think of it as a lifelong commitment. Marriage to them is a terminal arrangement.

I would refuse to marry any couple who admitted that; who did not at least *intend* that their marriage should be for life. There was a time when we used to talk of marriage in a romantic and sentimental way. Perhaps that was naive. And perhaps the statistics on divorce reflect that naivety. Certainly there is less of that sort of talk nowadays. Now our talk is less romantic, more realistic. Some people even talk about marriage in a cynical way, like one of the characters in Robert Frost's poem, *The Death of the Hired Man*, who says that "home is the place where, when you have to go there, they have to take you in." Or like the artist who said that marriage is a dull meal with the dessert served first. Or the counsellor who said that the human race could be divided into two groups; those who are convinced that all their problems would disappear if they were married and those who are absolutely certain that all their problems would be solved if they weren't!

There are others who do not feel like that; who went into marriage believing and expecting that it would get better, not worse; that they would grow to love each other more, not less; that the bond of marriage would enlarge and enhance, not diminish, their development. Is that naive? Is it foolish to want to die still married to the one to whom you pledged love long ago, and to love them more and cherish them better as the years go by?

Dare I offer a prescription for happiness at home? Who am I to do so? And yet, I would be pretty dull if I did not learn something from the experience of others; from members of congregations who have been trustful enough to come and share their experience of home and married life with me. I would be stupid if I didn't learn something from my own experience too. Remember, I am offering a *prescription*, not a cure. There is a difference. A cure is a guarantee. A prescription, if followed, holds out the possibility of improvement. A prescription also requires cooperation. You have to be willing to take it. My prescription for happiness at home has five ingredients.

The first thing is to realize that the happiness of at least two people is in your hands. The happiness of you and your partner; your husband or your wife. The Irish poet, W. B. Yeats, would correct me. He would say that the happiness of two people is not in your hands, it is under your feet. "I have spread my dreams under your feet," says the poet, "Tread softly, for you tread on my dreams."

Understand that another person, with one brief life, has entrusted his or her happiness to you. Their happiness, as well as your own, is in your hands or spread beneath your feet. One reason why this is so is that whatever we do, we usually do it for one person. However famous we are, however accomplished in our profession, whoever lavishes us with adulation, it is meaningless, it is dust and ashes, unless in the end we have the approval of the one person who matters most to us. If we have that person's good opinion, if we have their encouragement, sympathy, understanding and support, then nothing is too hard for us. But if we do not, our initiative is drained. Our courage is diminished. We lose our nerve. We are then only half the person we might be.

Think back to when you were a child! Can't you remember how your childish accomplishments meant nothing to you without your mother's smile? Whatever other people said, it was what your mother or father thought about it that mattered. You needed their approval, and wanted to feel their pleasure in your little accomplishments. It's sad that some children grow up without ever having felt that sense of being cherished and approved of. I think of Leslie Weatherhead, who, as an adult, discovered that his mother had never wanted him. All his childhood had been filled with anxiety, as he both feared his mother and longed for her love at the same time. And yet he was never sure he had it. I think of Arturo Toscanini, who, as a child, never knew whether or not his mother loved him. When he grew up and received the acclaim of vast audiences everywhere, he still felt this gnawing emptiness, this chasm in his soul. He could never be sure that his success brought any joy or comfort to his mother's heart. All our life we look for recognition or commendation from the one person who matters most to us in life.

Think of your husband. Think of your wife. That person, and that life, is in your hands. One frail, fragile, fleeting life, one person's happiness, has been linked and entrusted to you. So your support, concern, understanding and sympathy are as vital to that person's well-being as their encouragement and acceptance are to yours.

I think of two different men, Thomas Carlyle, and R. W. Dale. Thomas Carlyle's wife adored him. She said that the least attention from him glorified her. But one day she said to him, "Don't you think that an occasional word of praise to me would not be amiss?" Carlyle blazed at her in anger and said, "What's wrong with you woman, do you need to be praised for doing your duty?" I contrast that story with a story told of R. W. Dale of Birmingham, a shy, sensitive man who was among the greatest preachers of his own or any time. By temperament and inclination he was ill-fitted for controversy, yet he found himself the target of bitter hostility, hated for saying what he believed. And one day somebody asked him how he managed to survive. Dale replied very simply, "I am happy at home." When we find strength, encouragement and assurance at home we are enabled to fight dragons and kill giants because we know a place of refuge, a place of healing and of love. So, the first ingredient in my prescription is basic and fundamental. Think of your husband or your wife and say to yourself, that person's happiness is in my hands or, if you like, their dreams are spread under my feet. Tread softly!

The second ingredient is to understand what Jesus meant when He said that when people marry they become one flesh. That doesn't just mean that they become one flesh physically, though of course it does mean that. It means much more than that. It means that their lives are thereafter intertwined. It means that the well-being of one is inextricably bound up with the well-being of the other; so inseparably close are they that when one weeps the other tastes salt. That is what marriage means. That is what "one flesh" means. It follows from this that one partner must not put the other one down. Why? Because if you diminish your partner, you diminish yourself. You cannot lessen your partner's worth without lessening your own worth, because you are one flesh. For one to denigrate the other diminishes both.

Being one flesh means that you do not compete. Marriage is a partnership not a competition. If spouses compete and one wins, in reality, they both lose. J. B. Priestly pointed out that our society has gone mad on competition. It *is* a kind of madness. He says that we sometimes force artists to compete against themselves. We listen to Debussy and we say, is this piece of his music as great as that piece of his music? Sometimes we even make members of the same family compete with each other. I knew a professional man whose son was in the same profession and the father was jealous of his own son. He was so jealous that he belittled his son at every opportunity. Can you believe it? The sadness of it is that now his son is dead, and the father must live with the torment of how he had always tried to make his son appear inferior.

We even force our children to compete for our affection. Our gifted children minister to our own egos and we love them for it and speak of them proudly, in the most glowing terms. Often we do not speak of our less gifted children in that way. I remember more than thirty years ago going into a farmhouse in County Fermanagh, Northern Ireland. The scene is indelibly etched on my mind. I remember it as clearly as if it happened yesterday. There was a little boy there, whittling away on a piece of wood with a penknife. His mother began to talk to me about the boy and about his brother. She said, "This is the dull one." And the more she talked disparagingly of him, the smaller he got. She told me that the bright son was at school; he was academically inclined, and stood at the head of his class. But this wee fellow sitting by the hearth was stupid. He wasn't good at anything. So he sat there whittling away and being wounded by every sentence that this silly, unkind woman spoke. Before I left the farmhouse, I went over and looked at the piece of wood the "stupid" boy had been whittling. I couldn't have carved anything as beautiful if I had worked at it for ten years. This little fellow could become a master carpenter. One day he might be a great sculptor, yet his own mother dismissed him as useless because he could not compete with his more bookish, brilliant brother.

Sometimes we say that we should love our children equally. But the truth is that we do not love our children equally. How could we? We can't love them equally because they aren't equal. But we can do something even better than that. We can love them uniquely. Each one for what he is, without having to compete with the others for our love. So, in a marriage, if husband and wife compete, it will ensure that both lose. Marriage is a partnership not a competition.

Thomas à Kempis said a marvellous thing when he said that "the humble in spirit dwell in a multitude of peace." If you have a competitive spirit, and especially if you have it at home, you will not dwell in a multitude of peace. When husband and wife become one flesh, when they cherish each other instead of competing with each other, then they are not rivals, but partners and their peace is multiplied.

The third thing to notice is that no one person can meet all the needs of any other person. Your wife is not going to meet all your needs. Your husband is not going to meet all your needs.

Sometimes we think human character and personality are so rich that one person has everything and will meet all the expectations of another person. That is never true. No one person is endowed with all gifts and graces. If we enter marriage with that expectation, we are bound to be disappointed and our disappointment will lead to resentment, and resentment to restlessness until we say, "I really made a mistake. If only I had married Mary instead of Joan!" Or, "If I had not married George but had married John instead, everything would be different, and I should be much happier!" Well, things would be different. A different partner would have a different set of gifts and graces. But neither John nor Mary nor anyone else would have all the gifts needed to satisfy us, and we should still be left with unmet needs of one sort or another.

I recently read the Church magazine of a church I know well, and there was in it a kind of rogues' gallery of past ministers. Each minister had a paragraph describing his gifts and graces and what he had been able to accomplish during his ministry there. I noticed two ministers, one of whom had followed the other in the pastoral charge. Of the first minister the writer said that he was all heart. Of the second minister, the article said that he was all head. One minister deeply touched the congregation's feelings and emotions. It was a great change when the next minister came along and appealed primarily to their intellect and reason. But the marvellous thing about the magazine was that it appreciated both of them. It could so easily have been the other way. Instead of mentioning the things that each did well, the magazine could have given its attention to their deficiencies, complaining that one wasn't emotional enough, and the other wasn't intellectual enough. But it didn't. It made the most of their strengths, not their weaknesses. Our marriages must be like that magazine. So often wives and husbands come to me and say, "Well, he doesn't do this," or "she doesn't do that." The fact is that nobody does it all. If that's what we are looking for, then we are certain to be disappointed.

The Stoics can be of help to us on this point. Epictetus had a saying, "Everything has two handles. By one handle you can carry it, by the other you cannot." True wisdom comes from discovering which handle will carry whatever it is we are trying to carry. You will not carry your marriage by the qualities your partner doesn't possess. That is impossible. But you can carry it, and carry it successfully, by the qualities that *are* there, by affirming the strengths and attributes of your partner.

Now here is the fourth thing. A good marriage needs shared values. This does not mean that husband and wife must always be interested in the same things. There is a great variety of things we can do which nevertheless reflect common values. A woman may love to work in her garden for the joy of making things grow. Her husband may serve on a committee concerned with the effects of acid rain. These two people are doing different things but their values are the same. Each is affirming the value of conservation.

If there are not common values, there is bound to be conflict. Here is a materialist who thinks the most important thing in life is money and he is married to a person whose basic values are human and spiritual. Conflict is unavoidable. We must know what we are after, what we seek in life and marriage. Somebody said once that our hungers are the vital part of our character. What do you hunger for? What are you after? What do you believe life is all about? When you have discovered that, then marry someone whose values are compatible with and not opposed to your own. G.K. Chesterton remarked that if a landlady was renting a room the first question she should ask a prospective tenant is "Sir, what is your total view of the Universe?" He thought it important for a landlady to know her tenant's basic values!

Worship, the church, and the Christian faith can play a very important part in shaping our values. Worship just means worthship, to ascribe worth, and to worship is a way of declaring what you believe to be of supreme worth in your life. When we worship together it means that Sunday by Sunday we are confronted by certain values; values of truth, beauty, integrity, justice and love, all of which can bind a life or a marriage together. That is why I am so sad and impatient when a father says to a mother, "You look after the religious side of family life. You take care of that, I am not interested in it." Or when a wife says the same sort of thing to her husband. When a family worships together, and when both father and mother take religion seriously, they discover common values around which to build their own character, and the quality of their home life is enriched.

Here is the next ingredient. In a marriage, making love should really make love. William James used to say that when we express an emotion, we strengthen it. When we express love we don't merely express how we already feel; we increase our capacity for loving. By expressing our love we have deepened and strengthened it. If that is true in our marriage, then it means that making love is more than just having sex. Making love should literally *make* love.

I saw a TV show a few weeks ago in which a woman was invited to go to bed with a man who was not her husband. At one point she asked him, "Do you love me?" He answered, "What's that got to do with it?" I think it's got everything to do with it. Having sex may be an isolated moment in which we devour somebody else to satisfy an animal urge. But that is not making love. Making love is not an isolated, unrelated moment in a relationship. It is like a wave of the sea which cannot be separated from all the waves that precede it and come after it. Do you know what we call these other waves? We call them respect and affection and kindness and friendship and faithfulness and sensitivity. These are the waves that precede making love, and when they do precede it, love is increased. By loving each other, we come to love each other more.

Sometimes our love-making makes babies. That's another way in which making love actually makes love, because we love the babies and they love us and the amount of love in our lives is multiplied. I came into this world because my parents loved each other. I was literally loved into existence. Our children came into the world because my wife and I love each other and we loved them into existence. Think of it! God's creative activity is love, and when we join in that activity we may love another human soul into life and being. That is why the "How to do it" sex manuals are of limited usefulness, though they do have a certain comic value. They are long on technique and short on substance. For without genuine caring and affinity of mind and spirit, making love is an empty process. It ceases to be making love and becomes having sex.

Bertrand Russell, who was so clever in many ways and such a fool in some others, once said that on the honeymoon what a couple needed most was experience. What rubbish! What a honeymoon couple needs more than experience is a sense of humour, a sense of fun, and much, much caring.

When we make love with another person the product should be love. This means, too, that when, for one reason or another, love is refused, it should be refused with as much delicacy, tenderness, kindness, understanding and humour as are used whenever it is bestowed. If either husband or wife is insensitive in this matter, the sense of rejection they create can spoil the relationship and create humiliation and resentment.

This brings me to the fifth ingredient in my prescription. It is that while with friends we say, "the more the merrier," with husband and wife we say "two is company, three is a crowd." Nowadays this assertion is strongly challenged. Some say it is acceptable to have what they call "satellite relationships." That's a fancy word for adultery. The next time you hear someone promoting the acceptability of satellite relationships or extra-marital affairs, don't just listen to their exhortation, examine their lives. How did their theory work out in practice?

Again, Bertrand Russell's case is instructive. He was forever engaging in affairs and promoting the virtues of free love. But read his autobiography. You will discover that this man who talked so much about sexual liberation was consumed by anguish and jealousy and grief because neither he nor his partners could cope with the pain of the other's unfaithfulness.

There are certain intimacies that cannot be indiscriminantly shared. One of the greatest gifts that a husband can offer to his wife, or a wife to her husband, is the gift of faithfulness. And you can make the gift of faithfulness because your partner's faithfulness makes it possible. We men say we have been faithful to our wives as though that were a great accomplishment on our part. I feel quite sure that our faithfulness owes far more to their love and understanding than it owes to any virtue in us.

Here is another ingredient of my prescription! Husbands and wives sometimes neglect each other and lavish all their love on their children. I believe the best thing a father can do for his children is to cherish their mother. And the best thing a mother can do for her children is to love their father.

When I was growing up there were two things of which I was absolutely certain. I couldn't have articulated them then, but their certainty went deeper than thought. The first was that my parents loved me. There was no question about that. They loved me deeply and unconditionally. That was the steel-and-granite foundation of my being. The other thing I knew was that they loved each other. That was an even deeper security. It was not just that they loved me, although they did; it was that they loved one another. And in their love for each other I found security and peace. So if a woman neglects her husband for her children, she is doing her children a great disservice. And the best thing a father can do for his children is to love their mother.

When I perform the marriage ceremony I often think that the most precious words in the promises that are made are the words "to love and to cherish." What does it mean to cherish? First, I tried to define it myself. This is what I came up with: It means to value highly, to nurture with tenderness, to respect someone as infinitely and uniquely precious. I thought that was a pretty good definition. But then I turned to the Oxford Dictionary. There I found a sentence, or a phrase, I never thought I would find in a dictionary. Do you know what it says? It says, "To cherish is to hold in one's heart." I can't improve on that. So the next time you are at a wedding service, and you hear those words, here is what I suggest you do. While the bride and groom are making their vows to each other, why don't you very quietly and in your own place renew your own marriage vows. And when you say the word "cherish" remember that it means "to hold in one's heart." When fathers and mothers cherish each other, children know a wonderful sense of security and permanence.

That brings me to the last part of my prescription. Parents should show their children at least as much respect as they show their children's friends.

Isn't it true that when our children bring their friends to our home, we are unfailingly polite and considerate? Indeed, we show them more consideration than we afford our own children. C. S. Lewis describes having dinner with a family in which the father treated his children's opinions with impatience and contempt. The whole experience filled Lewis with anger at the man's rudeness and led him to observe that the close relations in a family demand an extraordinary degree of courtesy and consideration. When the children of our heart are treated with contempt, the whole family is diminished. When our children are honoured, they bring a unique strength to the "inner circle of those most dear." Parents need to remember that respect is an essential ingredient of love. Paul tells us that love is "not arrogant or rude." Just see how your children will grow in dignity and in their sense of personal worth when you not only love them but respect them!

Well, there's the prescription! It is far from perfect; but it doesn't need to be perfect. It just needs to be taken seriously. Make a new start with it, and see what it will do for you!

TRIVIAL PURSUIT

"What will a man gain by winning the whole world, at the cost of his true self? Or what can he give that will buy that self back?"
St. Matthew 16:26

A couple of summers ago, some people who used to be our friends taught us how to play *Trivial Pursuit*, and we have played it occasionally ever since. As you probably know, it is a game of questions. You are asked a question and if you get the right answer you are rewarded by being asked another question. And so it goes on, and as long as you keep on answering correctly, you move around the board.

Now I shouldn't want you to think that it is very profound. I know some people who decided to learn all the questions and answers off by heart, and that's what they did, but they are not much wiser than they were. In a sense the game is a sign of our time. You remember how T. S. Eliot asked, "Where is the wisdom we have lost in knowledge? Where is the knowledge we have lost in information?" *Trivial Pursuit* is just a matter of facts and information. Not wisdom, but facts without meaning. It really is trivial.

Maybe I should give you a couple of examples of the questions. Are you ready?

How many fingers did Anne Boleyn have?

What was Hitler's favourite movie?

What famous Hollywood film star was the seventh cousin of the Princess of Wales, Lady Diana?

Notice the fascination of the game! Once the question is asked it doesn't matter how trivial it is, you simply have to hear the answer. What would you do if I didn't tell you the answers to those questions? Some of you wouldn't sleep tonight! Once the question

95

is asked, we are hooked; we simply *must* satisfy our curiosity.

But there is another trivial pursuit, far more pervasive, far more mischievous than that. There is a trivial pursuit which is written into the second draft of the American Declaration of Independence. It says that it is the inalienable right of everyone to pursue happiness.

Now I have called that a trivial pursuit, but is it really fair to do so? After all, there are some senses in which the pursuit of happiness is not trivial. It certainly wasn't a trivial pursuit for those who shaped, and then reshaped, the American Declaration of Independence. For them it was an inalienable right conferred by God. It had to do with the whole matter of God's loving intention for your life and mine. They understood human happiness in our right relation to God. They related it to transcendent reality and eternal values. To conceive happiness as God's purpose for your life and mine is not at all trivial but goes to the very heart of who we are and why we are here.

And it certainly wasn't a trivial pursuit for a man who was, I suppose, the least trivial of men — John Wesley. Samuel Johnson used to complain that you could never keep Wesley long enough in one place to have a decent conversation. He was always going off to do something which he considered to be more important. Nothing trivial about Wesley! And yet it is Wesley who tells us that "faith is in order to goodness, as goodness is in order to love, as love is in order to happiness." Yes, happiness! In other words, it was no trivial pursuit because it had to do with nothing less than a right relationship with God our Creator, and our love for other people. There is nothing trivial about that!

There is another sense in which I think the pursuit of happiness is not a trivial pursuit. It's not trivial because of what it costs. The cost of it is very high. In the end, it costs us everything we have. It costs us our life. Every day another twenty-four hours is spent in the pursuit of what it is we are really after, what makes our wheels go round, what we think life is really about. And in the end, it costs us all our days and all our years and everything we have. Maybe I ought not to say it *will* cost you that. Perhaps I should tell you what it has cost you already.

Let us suppose, for example, that our life lasts for seventy years. Now, thank God it often goes on for much longer than that. But let us imagine just for the purposes of this sermon that our human life-span is the three-score years and ten the Bible mentions. Suppose, then, that we were to compress those seventy years into the waking hours of one day, say from seven in the morning until eleven at night. Let me tell you what your dream, your pursuit of happiness, has already cost you.

If you are fifteen years old, then it is twenty-five past ten in the morning.
If you are twenty-five, it is twelve forty.
If you are thirty, it is ten minutes to two.
If you are forty, it is a little after four.
If you are forty-five, it is a quarter past five.
If you are fifty, it is six twenty-five.
If you are fifty-five, it is twenty-five minutes to eight.
If you are sixty, it is twenty minutes to nine.
If you are sixty-five, it is ten minutes to ten.
And we all run out of time just as the news comes on at eleven!

One of the most beautiful poems ever written was written by Thomas Beddoes, and he called it *Dream Pedalry*. The poet begins by asking, "If there were dreams to sell, what would you buy?" And then he goes on to tell us what dreams cost. But there *are* dreams to sell, and everybody buys them. There are as many dreams as there are people. But they all cost the same amount, for in the end they cost us our life. And that isn't trivial.

But I suppose if that is true, then there are some other questions we ought to ask ourselves about this trivial pursuit. For example, if the pursuit of happiness costs us that much, then we ought to ask whether or not we are getting value for what we are paying.

Benjamin Franklin never forgot the ·first purchase he ever made. It was a tin whistle. When he was a little child he saw it in a store window and coveted it, and finally got the money and went and bought it. And almost as soon as he had purchased it, he knew he had been cheated. It had cost him too much. It wasn't worth what he had paid for it. But if he paid too much for the whistle, he didn't pay too much for the lesson it taught him. It stayed with him all through his life. And ever after he would look at men and women, friends and acquaintances, politicians and statesmen, absorbed in the pursuit of power, or fame, or wealth, and all getting too little for what it was costing them, and he would say to them, "You are paying too much for your whistle!" What a quaint little phrase! How much are you paying for your whistle?

Occasionally I watch television, and once or twice have seen a television game-show called *The Price is Right*. The producers of the show gather a crowd of hysterical materialists into a studio and then they show them things like cars and refrigerators and furniture, and invite the contestants to guess the price. The one who comes closest to the price wins the car or refrigerator or furniture.

The Price is Right is television at its worst. But it is more than a game. In fact, it is often what we do in life. What we do is put a value on things and then go after them. Is the price right? Do we take cheap, shoddy things and put a high value on them? Do we take life's truly precious things and value them cheaply? Questions of this sort ought to remind us of the meaning and importance of worship. Do you know what worship means? It means to ascribe worth. It simply declares the values which we affirm to be of supreme worth in life, so that true worship is to put the right value on the right thing. Someone said once that the whole purpose of education is to teach us to value what *ought* to be valued. That is certainly the purpose of worship; to ascribe worth to what is truly worthy.

There is a television commercial which I think is a splendid one. In it, a man tells us that "There are some people who know how to spend but don't know how to buy." They can get rid of their money, but what they get for it isn't much good. What they get for all their spending isn't worth buying. They pay too much for their whistle. I can put that same truth in words of Scripture. The Prophet Isaiah asked the question, "Wherefore do you spend your money for that which is not bread and your labour for that which satisfieth not?" That's even better than the man on television!

It leads me to the next question which asks, "If you are spending your money for that which is not bread and your labour for that which satisfieth not," how long are you going to allow yourself to be deceived? It seems to me that there are two ways in which we allow ourselves to be deceived, and the first of them is that we are afraid of failure. We set our goals of happiness and success, and we become totally absorbed in reaching them. We scratch and claw and shove to get what it is we are after, without stopping long enough to say, "But if I get it, is it really worth it, and is it what I really want?"

We are like the man with the mud-rake in *Pilgrim's Progress*, who keeps looking down, and doing his job, but never looks up to see the stars, or the clouds, or the sky. He knows nothing higher than the mud and himself. That's what we do. We keep our heads down, our noses to the grindstone, and keep on working to succeed. We never ask ourselves the question, "Suppose I do succeed, is what I'm after what I really want?" How sad it is that so many people who are successful in their business, or their profession, or their career have a sense that while they have succeeded in making a living, they have failed life! They have achieved success, and their success is their punishment.

Look, you young people, all bright-eyed and bushy-tailed, here is a good thought for you. When you feel you have got life by the throat, that you are going to get exactly what you want, be sure that what you want is worth the having. Why? Because I can't think of a better definition of hell than to have everything you ever wanted, and still to be unsatisfied. Make sure that the things you pursue are worthy of you.

So one of the most important things I could say to you is, "For goodness sake know what your basic principle is, what it is you are after in life." Because that basic principle is going to determine the nature of your gathering in and you mustn't expect from life more than your basic principle can deliver. Does that sound very difficult? Let me make it absolutely clear!

If you put self at the centre, you had better be prepared to find your outer limits there, and that can be very lonely. If what you are after is power, you had better forget about affection, it is very difficult to have both. If the goal of your life is security, you had better forget about ecstasy. If what you are really interested in is justice and not mercy, you had better not make mistakes. If you think that life is purely quantitive, you had better keep your averages up. If you think that life is a rat-race, you must not complain of a lack of dignity. If you think that your children are your personal possession, then you mustn't look for free, spontaneous and creative spirits. If your basic method is to manipulate, don't expect anybody to trust you. If you are a gossip, do not look for confidences. If you really are a materialist, you mustn't consult us gurus about spiritual values, for we have little to say to you, and even less that you would understand. If your basic method is one of confrontation, don't expect people to knock on your door when what they need is tenderness. If you decide to live by the sword, then by God you had better carry one. Do you know why? Because life is moral! It is not that business is moral or that the church is moral or that religion is moral. It is that *life* is moral. You really do reap what you sow. God is not mocked, for the last word is always His. So know what your basic principle is because it is going to determine the nature of your gathering in. You mustn't expect more from life than your basic principle can deliver.

Do you remember that marvellous film, *The Bridge on the River Kwai?* Alec Guinness played the Senior British Officer in a Japanese concentration camp and he undertook on behalf of the prisoners to build a bridge, a railway bridge, for the Japanese. He thought that this would lift his men's sagging morale and give them a sense of purpose, something to accomplish. It did all of those things. They built the bridge. Indeed, they built it so well that the Allies had to organize an expedition to blow it up; and when the Senior British officer saw that they were trying to destroy his achievement, he was outraged. Then there comes the terrible moment in which Alec Guinness realizes what has happened, and he cries out, "My God, what have I done?" He was so busy succeeding in his enterprise that he lost all sense of its *meaning*. He had built a bridge for the enemy!

We do it all the time. We are so busy trying to succeed that we lose our sense of what success means. We are so afraid of failure that we devote all our energies to what we have undertaken and then, having achieved it, having come through it all successfully, we ask ourselves what we have done. It is not what we wanted. It is not enough to satisfy. We have built a bridge for the enemy and our success is our punishment.

We deceive ourselves in another way. We say, "Well, maybe

what I have now doesn't satisfy me, but if I had more, it would. If I could just get another five-hundred dollars a month, that would be enough. Maybe not this house, but another house. Not this woman, but another woman. Not this church, but another church." I know some ministers who are never in the church they are in. They are always in the next one, the better one, the perfect one. And so it is we go on telling ourselves that more of the same will accomplish what a little has failed to do. It won't!

Be utterly sure about this. This is a word that comes to you not only from my own experience, and from the New Testament, but from some of my friends whose work it is to study career patterns and business success. What they say is that if what you are doing now gives you no satisfaction, more of the same won't do it. If you are not finding your fulfillment in what you are now doing, it won't be any better when you get the boss's office, where the carpet goes all the way to the wall and there is a bigger desk. They urge us never to commit our happiness to the future, because it doesn't work. It's a very good thing for the physician to write "repeat the prescription" if the medicine is working. But if it isn't, then to repeat the prescription is foolish.

When we arrived in Canada from Ireland in 1959 we came to First United Church in Hamilton. One of the most enjoyable things about First United was the couples' club, and one of the club's highlights was its annual auction sale. Nobody took it very seriously. Everybody gathered up their accumulated junk and sent it down to the church. They brought in a professional auctioneer for the occasion. He sold all this stuff and the event raised some money for missionaries and the club budget. Well, two of our friends in Hamilton, Joe and Mildred, had some old lawn furniture that had been lying about on the verandah. Mildred thought the auction sale a marvellous opportunity to get rid of it. So she sent it all off to be sold. But when the time came for the auction, Mildred was ill and couldn't go. Joe went instead. You guessed it! Joe saw this lawn furniture and bought it. He thought he had found a terrific bargain. Poor Mildred! She had to wait another year to get rid of the stuff. How we laughed over that! But sometimes we do the same thing in life. We ask the question, "Do you buy it?" Friends, we not only buy it, we buy it back! We fall again for the promises that have proved empty, the values that are not great enough to satisfy us.

Now, so far I have tried to show that happiness and the pursuit of it are not trivial. But I called this sermon "Trivial Pursuit," and I want to end by telling you why the pursuit of happiness *is* a trivial pursuit.

It is a trivial pursuit because we try to find our happiness in trivial things. There isn't any harm in going after happiness if we can see that it is God's loving intention for us, and if we seek it in Him. It becomes trivial when we seek it by going after trivial things. By values that are too small for us. Somebody said once that the human spirit can't rest in things beneath itself. I hope that is true! Wouldn't it be sad to think that ordinary things like money and property and sex and power would be enough to satisfy the human spirit? What poor creatures we should be if that were the truth of us! Is it not true that you were made for beauty and loveliness and goodness and for those ultimate values without which the human spirit shrivels and dies?

Happiness need not be trivial, but when we wrench this phrase, "The Pursuit of Happiness" from the American Declaration of Independence, and make it into something purely materialistic, it *becomes* trivial. When we equate happiness with pleasure or power or sex, or when we feel it gives us a God-given right to exploit and to plunder and to do whatever we choose so long as we are happy, then that is a trivial pursuit.

One of the most powerful plays I have seen is Marlowe's *Dr. Faustus.* You remember how Faustus, Doctor of Divinity, wearies of his studies and decides to make a deal with Satan. And so he draws a magic circle on the ground and in the circle writes Jehovah's name and conjures up old Lucifer complete with sulphur and all the noise of hell. And so the deal is made. He gets twenty-five years of near-absolute power, and at the end of it, must surrender his soul. Having got this power, what does poor John Faustus do with it? Let me tell you. He has grapes out of season! He makes fun of the Pope! He goes to bed with Helen of Troy; he sees "the face that launched a thousand ships and burnt the topless towers of Ilium." All this he does, and it costs him his soul. Grapes out of season? But you and I can buy them any day at the nearest supermarket! To make fun of the Pope? But Ian Paisley does that regularly. To go to bed with

Helen of Troy? But don't you know many a man who lost his soul for a pretty face? This trivia at the cost of his own soul! This is what John Faustus, who knew something of divinity but little of God, did with his power. Trivial pursuits!

One of the great plays of our time is Robert Bolt's *A Man for All Seasons*. Do you remember how Sir Thomas More with wit and charm and grace and wisdom managed to preserve his life without losing his integrity? Because he knew his dimensions, where he began and where he left off; what he was prepared to surrender and what he wasn't. And then at the end, he is done in by Richard Rich, a little worm of a man, who lies under oath and whose lie is Thomas More's death warrant. Sir Thomas knows he is a dead man. And for his lie Richard Rich is made Attorney-General of Wales. That was the prize. And in the play Sir Thomas sees Richard Rich wearing his chain of office. Thomas More instructs his betrayer in the cost and triviality of worldly power. "For Wales?" he asks. And goes on, "Richard, it profits a man nothing to give his soul for the whole world . . . But for Wales."

We all do it! And for much less than Wales! Our search for happiness is a trivial pursuit because we have trivialized it by going after trivial things. Malcolm Muggeridge, who better perhaps than any contemporary writer has expressed the false values of Western Civilization, writes of driving into an American city late at night and seeing the flashing neon lights around him. One said, "Food"; the next said said, "Gas"; the next said "Beauty"; and the last said "Drugs". Food, Gas, Drugs and Beauty. Muggeridge realized that here were the trivial pursuits of our time; and not just of North America, but of the whole world.

G. K. Chesterton had a similar experience. He visited New York and stood in Times Square with all the neon messages being flashed to him. Someone asked him what he thought of it and Chesterton replied, "It would be marvellous if only one couldn't read!" What energies we all squander in the pursuit of trivia!

That brings me to the final point. The pursuit of happiness is trivial because the harder we pursue it the less chance we have of getting it. I love that! Do you know why? Because it is God's great joke. Do you remember the couplet by Robert Frost,

Forgive, O Lord, my little jokes on Thee
And I'll forgive Thy great big joke on me!

God's great big joke is that there are some things you can't get by going after them. The harder you try, the further you are from getting them. They come by what C. S. Lewis once called "the principle of inattention." In other words, they can be yours only when you are not looking for them. Suddenly you are in Wordsworth's great phrase, "Surprised by Joy." That's the essence of it. I know all kinds of people who are desperately trying to be happy. And they are the most miserable people I know. But when you are doing something else, writing a book, or painting a picture, or talking with your friends, or loving your wife or children, then silently, surreptitiously, happiness surprises you. Haven't you experienced that? You were engaged in some worthwhile task, devoting all your energy to it, when to your utter astonishment you were surprised by joy. It was there unsought, God's good gift, bestowed when least expected. Sydney Smith, who was a very wise man and, incidentally, a clergyman, wrote these words, "Many in this world run after felicity like an absent-minded man hunting for his hat, while all the time it is there on his head or in his hand." Have you noticed how many important things in life are like that? Have you noticed that people who are trying hard to be original never are? Those who are trying to be original aren't even interesting! But forget about being original, and do your best work, and you might be surprised at how original you are!

Somebody came to me once and asked, "How do I get culture?" Well, I don't know how you get culture. I suspect that the one way *not* to get it is to go after it. If you are really trying to get it then you are going to miss it. Do you know why? Because when you go to the orchestral concert you are not really listening to the music, you are just looking at yourself listening to the music! And when you go to the art gallery to look at the pictures someone has told you are "great," you are not really looking at the pictures, you are looking at yourself looking at the pictures!

Have you ever tried to be humble? If you have ever *tried* to be humble you are in a spiritually hazardous condition! What are you if you succeed? Do you tell your friends, "I have done it! I am tops in humility!" You cannot *achieve* humility. Truly humble people never think of it; they're too busy thinking about more important and interesting things.

Goodness is like that. Try hard to be good and the chances are you will end up being self-righteous. Haven't you noticed that the people who are truly humble and who are truly good never think of their humility and goodness? Their minds are elsewhere. Do you really think that Mother Teresa is trying hard to be happy? Or Jean Vanier?

You can't have these qualities by going after them. You see, the truth is that you get them only when you are after something else, something ultimate. Do you know what that is? It is simply to know and love and serve God! And God's ultimate joke is that if you do that, you get everything else thrown in. C. S. Lewis wrote, "Look for yourself, and you will find in the long run only hatred, loneliness, despair, rage, ruin, and decay. But look for Christ and you will find Him, and with Him everything else thrown in." Jesus put it very simply, "Set your mind on God's Kingdom and His justice before everything else, and all the rest will come to you as well."

I have finished. But I must tell you that Anne Boleyn had eleven fingers. The seventh cousin of the Princess of Wales was Humphrey Bogart. Hitler's favourite movie was *King Kong*!

Trivial Pursuit! It's great fun. I hope you play it.

But not with your life!

A TALE OF TWO CITIES

"Those who use such language show plainly that they are looking for a country of their own. If their hearts had been in the country they had left, they could have found an opportunity to return. Instead, we find them longing for a better country — I mean, the heavenly one. That is why God is not ashamed to be called their God; for He has a city ready for them."

Hebrews 11:15,16

One of the most impressive things about the author of the Book of Revelation is his sense of belonging to two worlds at the same time. In the first chapter John declares that he "was in the Isle that is called Patmos, and in the Kingdom of Jesus Christ." He knows two Jerusalems: an "old" one that can be located on a map of Palestine, and the "new" Jerusalem, an Eternal City, which comes down from God out of heaven and whose citizens are gathered from every nation. Living in time, he knows himself a child of the Eternal; living in this world, his true home is a "Spiritual World" from which this world derives its meaning.

John's experience is the experience of every Christian. We are on the earth as strangers and pilgrims, seeking "a city which hath foundations, whose builder and maker is God." We belong to an eternal Kingdom and know the power and influence of the spiritual world all through our earthly pilgrimage. We, too, are "in the Isle that is called Patmos and in the Kingdom of Jesus Christ."

When Israel was in Babylonian exile, their captors required of them a song saying, "Sing to us one of the Songs of Zion," to which they received the understandable reply, "How can we sing the Lord's song in a strange land?" Understandable, as we have said; and yet there is a sense in which God's people have never done anything else but sing the Lord's song in a strange land. Or as John would say, we sing the songs of the heavenly Jerusalem while we are in the Isle that is called Patmos.

When William Wordsworth wrote a poem about a skylark, he observed that it rises from its nest upon the dewy ground into a glorious light, aspiring "to the last point of vision and beyond." It is, he tells us, "true to the kindred points of heaven and home."

Now that is precisely what we must discover. Citizens of two cities, of two Kingdoms, of two worlds, we must discover how to be true to both. For it is God's will that we should hold a dual citizenship, belonging at the same time to an earthly and a heavenly Kingdom, and that we should render to each an appropriate allegiance.

What, then, does our heavenly citizenship tell us about our earthly pilgrimage?

I. That the Spiritual World is the source of our adequacy.

The thing to notice about Patmos is that it wasn't just an island; it was a slave-camp. John was a prisoner when he wrote the words, sentenced to hard labour on the tiny, volcanic island. He was in Siberia, in Dachau, in Belsen. He was being persecuted by the Emperor Domitian, who stood astride the world like a Colossus and threatened with imprisonment and death those who declared the gospel of Jesus, the Christ.

Yet it was from that island and that man that there was heard a shout of praise, a paean of victory, a glorying in Christ that has left its mark on Christianity to this day. In *The Service Book* of the United Church of Canada, more than half of the Ascriptions of Glory come from the pen of this man. He was in Patmos, and the words have the sound of death. He was in the Kingdom of Christ, and the concentration camp was the very gate of heaven.

Now it is just this sense of belonging to another Kingdom, of having another King, that has enabled Christian people not only to endure, but to transform their hardships. The early martyrs strengthened each other by affirming that they would not be able to distinguish between the flash of the executioner's sword and the sheen of Christ's garments. Three hundred years ago Samuel Rutherford, a Scottish Covenanter, wrote from his prison in

Aberdeen, "Jesus Christ came into my cell last night and every stone flashed like a ruby."

I remember listening to a young missionary who had been imprisoned by the Chinese Communists. They kept him in solitary confinement. His Bible and hymnbook were taken from him. He did not receive enough food to eat. He was denied water to drink and with which to wash himself. Every night he was told that he would be shot the next morning. But into his cell, he tells us, there came a great cloud of witnesses; he says he knew for the first time what the Church means by "the Communion of Saints." Suddenly he felt there were thousands with him, and he knew the promise of God confirmed, that there is a special blessing for those who are persecuted for the sake of righteousness.

Now it is exactly this experience of inexhaustible grace that enabled the Apostle Paul to make the most astonishing and paradoxical claim. When he appeared to have nothing, he claimed to have everything; with no visible resources, he exulted with the confidence of one who had all that he needed. Listen to him:

We are the impostors who speak the truth,
The unknown men whom all men know.
Dying, we still live on,
Disciplined by suffering we are not done to death,
In our sorrows we have always cause for joy.
Poor ourselves, we bring wealth to many;
Penniless, we own the world.

I suppose our circumstances are unlike any of those we have described. We have never been imprisoned for our faith. To serve Christ has not meant, for us, hard labour on a barren island. Yet life makes great demands upon us, and our need for courage and hope, for wisdom and patience and grace is very great. John, who "was on the Isle of Patmos and in the Kingdom of Christ" declares that there are resources sufficient to supply our need. Our adequacy is not in ourselves but in God. We can do all things through Christ who strengthens us. We receive help and encouragement from the Eternal, Spiritual World:

And when the strife is fierce, the warfare long,
Steals on the ear the distant triumph-song,
And hearts are brave again, and arms are strong.
                                        Alleluia!

II. Our belonging to another Kingdom denies to this world and
this life any ultimate power over us.

Many of you know very well that life can bring sore trials, and
inflict terrible wounds. Suffering, sorrow, mental illness, disappointment, loneliness, come to many people and, of course, death
finally comes to all of us. John knows all these things; but he knows,
too, that they are not able to mute that last note of the triumph of
God. Their power is limited. The powers of this world can bring us,
on a dark night, to a place of crucifixion, but they cannot hold back
the resurrection dawn.

I remember talking to a man who in the early years of his
career, during the Great Depression, had a boss who tried to force
him into dishonest and sordid schemes and conspiracies which
served his boss's interest. For a time, life was a torment. Then one
day he realized that the worst his boss could do was fire him. Now
that was terrible enough, yet it was a deliverance for him to
remember it. His boss had some authority over him, but it was not
an ultimate power. It was severely limited. He couldn't rob him of
his wife's love, or the joy he found in his children, or his own self-
respect and integrity. He could take away his job, but having done
so, there was nothing more that he could do to hurt him.

The Apostle Paul faced the worst that life could do; he
deliberately brought together in one terrible array the powers that
confronted him, that threatened to possess and destroy him, and he
announced the limits of their power for they could not snatch him
from God's hands or separate him from the Divine love. In truth, he
did not belong to them, they belonged to him, for he, and every
Christian, could defeat them by the power and love of Christ.
"Everything belongs to you" he tells his fellow Christians, "The
world, life and death, the present and the future; all of them belong
to you, for you belong to Christ and Christ belongs to God." Jesus
said the same thing in different words when he told his disciples not
to fear those who could kill the body, for having done that they had

reached the limit of their power, and had done the worst that they could do. They had no power to put them beyond the reach of God's love or pluck them out of His hand.

Once, during the Nazi occupation, the unarmed people of Oslo stood outside their closed Cathedral and sang Luther's great hymn.

And though they take our life,
Goods, honour, children, wife,
Yet is their profit small:
These things shall vanish all,
The City of God remaineth.

Notice, too, that if this world has no ultimate power to destroy us, neither has it any ultimate power of happiness. We, who belong to another Kingdom, tell this one not only that it has no ultimate power to harm us, but that it cannot satisfy us.

In his book, *Jesus Rediscovered*, Malcolm Muggeridge, who has been everywhere, met everyone, and done everything, tells us that he has achieved fame, wealth, some measure of fulfillment in his work,and the means to indulge every appetite. "Let me tell you," he goes on, "that they mean nothing beside what Jesus Christ has to offer us. For me, it is Christ or nothing."

That reminds me of a man I met not long ago. He owns two Cadillacs; he has a magnificent home, a beautiful wife, and a talented family. He told me that as a boy he was poor and unhappy, and decided that when he grew up he would be rich and happy. Well, now he is rich, but he is unfulfilled, and has discovered that his children have already rejected his values and are busy making their own way without his money. Talking about his wealth he said, "It hasn't done what I thought it would do for me, and they don't want it." That man's experience confirms another of the ironies that Malcolm Muggeridge points out to us. He says that he has never met a rich man who was happy, or a poor man who didn't want to be rich!

Many of us don't really believe that. What we do believe is that if we had a larger salary, a better house, greater fame or more power, then we should be happy. We believe the television ad-men who assure us that if only we have the right brand of colour television, drive the right car, drink the right beer, wash with the right soap, brush with the right toothpaste, life will be wonderful. We should listen to those who possess and do all these things and who tell us that we can have them all and still have a life that is empty! Remember who tells us this! Believe those who already have what we spend our time trying to get, and who testify that the promises are not kept and the goods are never delivered. I am glad to be able to tell you this. Have you ever thought what pathetic creatures we should be if we could be satisfied by the poor material things I have mentioned? In advertising the products that make for happiness, the advertisers strip us of dignity. They show us to ourselves as gross creatures without heroism, or splendour, or a sense of beauty; satisfied with affluence, asking only for security, aspiring only to be comfortable. We must not allow them to make us forget "that Imperial Palace whence we came," for while we are on the Island of Patmos our true home is heavenly Jerusalem. Have you not felt the sadness in what is most lovely, a sadness that contains hints of perfect loveliness? Have you not found that every true joy here seems to point us away beyond itself to something more perfect and more joyous still? We are all members of that little band of wanderers who, as strangers and pilgrims upon the earth, are seeking another city which hath foundations, whose builder and maker is God. For there is nothing here that can satisfy us. So said John, who was in the Isle of Patmos and in the Kingdom of Christ.

III. Notice, next, that our belonging to another Kingdom enriches our appreciation of this life.

You see, it is only when we have put this world in its place, denying that it has any ultimate power to harm or satisfy us, that we can begin to appreciate it. Sometimes in the history of Christianity, those who have affirmed the reality of the spiritual world have denied the value of this world. They sang, "Earth is but a desert drear, heaven is my home." The joys of this life were regarded with suspicion, and sometimes avoided as sinful merely because they gave pleasure, not because they were intrinsically evil. What those Christians failed to appreciate is that this life is God's good gift to us, and that it is sheer ingratitude not to rejoice and be glad in it:

> The Puritan through life's sweet garden goes,
> And plucks the thorn and throws away the rose,
> He thinks to please by this peculiar whim,
> The God who made and fashioned it for him.

That was not true of all Puritanism, but it was true of some Puritans. They forgot that He has given us all things richly to enjoy; they failed to appreciate those magnificent words of Genesis, "And God saw everything that He had made, and behold, it was very good." I had a professor in college who used to say, "At the day of Judgement we shall be called to account, not only for those sins we have committed, but for those good gifts of God which we have not enjoyed." If Christians took that word to heart they would be far more winsome. One of Paul Tillich's complaints against the faith was simply that "The redeemed do not look redeemed!" The late Tom Clelland of Duke University described one of his Scottish professors as a Calvinistic Cassius whose face looked like the edge of a hatchet that had been dipped in vinegar! And who, having once read it, could ever forget Ibsen's *Julian* and his description of the Christians he knew? "Have you looked at these Christians closely?" he asks. "Hollow-eyed, pale-cheeked, flat-breasted all; they brood their lives away, unspurred by ambition; the sun shines for them, but they do not see it; the earth offers them its fullness, but they desire it not; all their desire is to renounce and suffer, that they may come to die."

Now one thrust of modern theology with which I concur is its emphasis on the Christian's celebration of the world; the created order, the beauty of changing seasons, the joy of human love, the rich treasures of art and music and literature. It invites us, as does the Bible, to face life with all its mystery and ambiguity, and to declare it good. For it is in this life that He shows Himself; and this world, charged with the grandeur of God, is the place of His self-disclosure. He took our flesh upon Him, and it was a human body that bore the weight of glory. Here is the sphere of our opportunity to love and serve others, to learn the meaning of compassion and the power of mercy. No Christian can ever call this world "a desert drear" or belittle its significance, for the Word became flesh, and God is present in this world which He created and which He loves.

By His Spirit He gives to this time and space an eternal significance; He glorifies matter, for it is His creation and bears His message.

IV. Our citizenship in heaven reminds us that our message is a Proclamation.

Some years ago I attended a missionary rally at which reports of the work of the church in many parts of the world were heard. Some were encouraging and some were disappointing. At the end, the choir rose to sing. Imagine what they sang! It was not, "O weary band of pilgrims." It was not, "Fight the good fight." It was not even "Jesus shall reign." They sang "Halleluiah! For the Lord God omnipotent reigneth, King of Kings and Lord of Lords."

Now it would be easy for the cynic to say that that triumphant music was the expression of a religion whose emotionalism is stronger than its logic. But the New Testament on every page declares that the triumph of God is no dream; it is *the* reality. God is on the Throne of the Universe and the Saviour is at His right hand in Glory. The final issue of things is not for a moment in doubt. He is King, and the last word and the final triumph belong to Him.

Now this makes all the difference to the task and the mood of the church. Our task is not to make Him King but to declare that He is King already. Even when men do not acknowledge Him, when they deny His Lordship and rebel against Him and seek to break their bands asunder, He is King, the Creator and Ruler of all things. Why, the very freedom by which men reject Him is theirs only because He wills that they should have it.

In Blake's poem, *Jerusalem*, he calls for his bow of burning gold, his arrows of desire and his chariots of fire, for his intention is nothing less than to build the New Jerusalem in England's green and pleasant land. The words are thrilling, and Parry set them to glorious music. And of course no Christian would wish to quarrel with the grandeur of the author's enterprise. But John on Patmos has something even greater to tell us. It is that while we may strive to build the New Jerusalem, the Eternal City does not depend upon our efforts. He tells us that it is not of our building; it is God's work, and God's gift, and it is already prepared;

And I, John, saw the New Jerusalem coming down from God out of Heaven, adorned as a bride for her husband.

The city which we seek and towards which we move is "a City which hath foundations, whose Builder and Maker is God." And the reality of His Lordship is neither threatened by human opposition nor dependent on human approval. That was John's secret. Behind Caesar was the Christ. Above Domitian, Jesus crowned! More eternal than Rome, the New Jerusalem! Beyond the Babylonian captivity, the joy of the Father's house! And that makes all the difference to our mood and confidence. The church is not merely militant, it is triumphant.

Thirty years ago, a layman was delivering his class-ticket to the richest man in town. Do you remember the class-ticket? It was like our Communion Card, and the Class-Leader was like our Elder. Poor himself, this Class-Leader had never been to such a grand house before. When the servant answered the front door, he saw this labouring man and said, "You must go round to the back." "Not so, not so," said the Class-Leader, "I'm here on the King's business."

We are on the King's business. We have nothing to be ashamed of when we offer Christ. There are many things in my own life, and in the church, which make me ashamed, but nothing in Jesus Christ. And He is King. In the end His love will be seen to be the only terms on which life is desirable or possible. At the last, every knee will bow and confess that He is Lord.

So said John, who "was in the Isle of Patmos and in the Kingdom of Jesus Christ."

"Praise and honour, glory and might, to Him who sits on the throne and to the Lamb for ever and ever!"

Amen

WHEN GOD LETS US DOWN

"Evil has come though I expected good."

Job 30:26

Job's bitter complaint against God is that his expectations have been dashed. He brings a charge against the Almighty implying that God has treated him cruelly. In words full of bewilderment and resentment he cries out, "Evil has come though I expected good."

Now when we turn to the Bible, that is not the kind of thing we look for. Our hope is that by reading it we shall find our faith in God strengthened and renewed. We expect to increase in confidence and joy through the message of the Scriptures, and that often happens. But it is to our profit to notice that the great pioneers of faith, those who in the end minister to our confidence and hope, are often those who are most petulant and dissatisfied with God. When we turn to the Bible we find that some of the heroes of the faith, people whom we hold up as examples, were distressed at God's way of doing things, and did not hesitate to say so. They called God to account. They said, "We don't like what you are doing! Why are you doing it?" So often it is the unbeliever who is polite with God. The real believer is often impolite because for him faith is a matter of life and death; so he demands that God should explain himself. Believers in Scripture call God to account and sometimes they are angry and bitter, and often they are bewildered. "What do you think you are doing?" they ask God. "What way is this to run the universe?"

Notice how this questioning attitude is to be found all the way through the Bible. Here is Moses, for example, who complains that God has given him a difficult task and hasn't really been much help to him in doing it. Here is Jeremiah who complains, "You called me when I was a child in my mother's womb, and on the strength of

117

your call I became a prophet. What did I discover? I find I am deceived! You have made a fool of me so that I am a scandal to my people who mock me, and mocking me, they mock you! What way is that to treat your servant?" Here is Habakkuk who is perplexed and confused by his experience of God and of life. He says that the trouble with God is that He has no regard for right or wrong. He does not care for human misery. If He really is God, why doesn't He do things differently?

I could multiply examples. Throughout the Scriptures we find men of great faith questioning or castigating God.

Notice that they fought that battle of faith not only for themselves, but for us. So if they fought it for us, we ought to know how they felt and what they said, and gather the benefit of their struggle into our expectation and our understanding of faith. But we seldom do. The reason we don't is that for many of us faith is not a matter of life and death, but rather a matter of habit and convention. Politeness toward God will suffice for most of us, most of the time. We tip our cap to Him. We enjoy a comfortable, easy relationship. Our happy expectation that He will take care of us goes on for years without being tested, for crises are few. We are pleased with God, and happy enough with the church. We have faith enough for life and life is easeful. Then we find ourselves in a predicament. A crisis. We may suddenly discover that faith is no longer a comfortable habit but a battlefield where, if we do not win, then the outcome will be defeat and despair. But if we have not considered what these great ones have said to us, then we have not prepared ourselves for the storm until it is too late. As an old Scottish crofter used to say, "The time to thatch your cottage is not in the storm but in the sunshine. Not when the wind is howling and the elements rage, but in the calm weather, so that when disaster strikes you find yourself prepared." We can do this without going outside the Book of Psalms. If we listen to what the psalmist said to God, we shall discover that he has much to say to us.

Notice, first, how there was a time when the psalmist's expectation was that good people would enjoy special privileges, obvious signs of the Divine favour. And why not? Doesn't it seem appropriate that when you are religious, God will be clearly on your side? Isn't it comforting to have "a Friend in High Places" to look after you? What can the providence of God mean if it doesn't mean that He loves those who love Him, and that He looks after His own? Are we not inclined to agree with the psalmist's expectation? Should there not be special privileges for those who are good?

Nor is the psalmist reticent or imprecise about his expectations; "A thousand shall fall at thy side, and ten thousand at thy right hand" he tells us, "but it shall not come nigh thee." There is no shortage of people to close with such an offer. Every week I meet those who suppose that because of their great faith or their special virtue, they will be recipients of Divine protection. They believe they are righteous and that God will look after them. They will not get cancer. They will not be unemployed. They will not lose dear ones in tragic accidents. Sometimes they share their expectations with me. When they are in hospital waiting for the results of tests, they say, "You know, Dr. Boyd, I am not worried. I have faith that God, who has been so good to me, will not allow me to get cancer." And when things turn out as they expect, they immediately relate the happy outcome to the greatness of their faith. This serves to strengthen their confidence that God will allow no evil to befall them. Indeed, I have known people to be not merely confident in their expectations, but arrogant in them. I have shuddered to think of the presumptuousness of their faith, and the pretentiousness underlying their claim to special protection by reason of their own virtue.

Such people seem never to stop and think of all the good people whose medical tests confirmed their worst fears, for whom the prognosis was grave. I know them and I minister to them. They too have faith. They too love God. Goodness has followed them all the days of their life. But now, suddenly, it's different. Evil has come when they expected good. Sometimes they lose dear ones, or they are worried about their children, or they lose their job, or their marriage goes sour. It is easy to have faith when the going is easy, but what about the other times?

I remember reading an article by Chaplain Stephen Webster, who was in Europe with the American Forces during the Second World War. It was an angry article called "Who Gets the Breaks in Prayer?" He told his readers that he was fed up with all the stories of miraculous rescues at sea and deliverances from rafts adrift in the North Atlantic; deliverances attributed by people to God in response to their great faith. Such incidents foster the idea that if only we are good and say our prayers, God will never let us down. He will look after us and do precisely what we ask Him to do. Chaplain Webster wanted to tell of the good men and women he knew who were not rescued. They prayed and they had faith, but they were not miraculously plucked from danger, but died, undelivered, yet still full of faith and trust.

The psalmist came to recognize the same truth that Chaplain Webster saw. He too discovered that bad things happen to good people, that virtue is no guarantee of safety, that the by-product of great faith is not necessarily great security. We must come alive to this truth just as the psalmist came alive to it. But notice that his first expectation was of special privileges for special people; that the good and the righteous and the virtuous would not be afflicted. But then the psalmist was disappointed in that expectation. He had to revise it with the truth of his own experience.

This was a painful process. He did not immediately discover the answer. Instead he found a middle position. He said, "Well, maybe it was too much to ask for special privileges for the godly. But surely they have a right to expect and receive justice." Again, we agree with him. Surely it is not unreasonable to expect what we deserve. In other words, the good should be rewarded according to their goodness, and the wicked punished according to their wickedness. That ought not to be too much to ask of God. If He has any sense of justice He must see that that is how He ought to order the universe. We may not have a right to special privilege, but surely we have a right to justice!

This expectation too is dashed. The psalmist discovers that, in the words of our Lord, our heavenly Father "makes His sun rise on good and bad alike, and sends the rain on the honest and the dishonest." God seems to be indifferent to justice, if one judges by His conduct. He doesn't seem to be as eager as we are to reward the good and punish the bad. The psalmist looks for fairness and doesn't get it and wonders why.

In this matter too we are like the psalmist. We often complain that life isn't just, and we are disappointed in God because we think that if He were good and loving He would demonstrate this by treating us fairly. I talked to a woman not long ago who had decided to leave the Christian church. Do you know why? Because she knew two people who were not treated as they deserved. One was a bitter old woman, sour and vicious and cranky, who for years had made everyone around her miserable. Yet she lived on and on, and every day she lived added more misery to the lives of those around her. The second person was a young man and a good one. He was kind and generous and sensitive so that everyone loved him. Wherever he went he brought strength and grace into people's lives. Suddenly he died and all his goodness was lost. This woman couldn't stand it. She complained bitterly to me that if God really cared about us, and if He were just, He would see to it that this kind of thing didn't happen. Why should the fine young man die young, and the embittered old woman go on and on? Like the psalmist she concluded that life isn't fair. It's not right that His sun should rise on good and bad alike, and His rain fall on the honest and the dishonest. He seems to be indifferent to good and evil, to have no regard for simple justice.

So the psalmist discovers that he has to give up his second expectation. He had been forced to abandon the prospect of special privilege, and now he has to abandon the expectation of simple justice. Then he goes on to make his bitterest observation. He discovers that his predicament is even worse than that. God has added insult to injury. It is not simply that there are no special privileges for the good. It is not merely that He seems indifferent to justice. The worst of all is that the wicked flourish! Read the psalmist's howl of indignation in Psalm 73. He is astounded. He cannot understand it. How can it be that the wicked prosper and get the breaks and the good things in life, while the virtuous, honest folk seem always to be struggling uphill?

Of course, one could argue against the psalmist. It would be easy to say that life is really not as unjust as he says it is; that he is selecting two or three instances of the wicked prospering and the good suffering, and drawing too general a conclusion. No doubt it is easy to exaggerate the prosperity of the wicked and the suffering of the virtuous.

But instead of quarrelling with the psalmist, let us allow his point. There is something in what he says, because wickedness, by its very nature, has an advantage over goodness. A liar has an advantage over a truthful person. The unscrupulous person, because he is unscrupulous, has a competitive edge over the man or woman of high principles. Reinhold Niebuhr wrote about this years ago. He called his book, *The Children of Light and the Children of Darkness*. He wrote about totalitarian regimes and democratic societies. He pointed out that totalitarian regimes have a real advantage in negotiating treaties because they have scant regard for truth. They can say anything that suits their purpose. But those countries whose leaders take their promises seriously must be careful about the treaties they sign. Similarly, religious cults in our society which seek to capture and twist the minds of our young people have an advantage; for the very qualities which we seek to inculcate in our children are precisely the qualities which make them vulnerable to the cults. We have taught our children a high regard for truth, to respect religious leaders, to treat the opinions of others with tolerance, not to close their minds to new truth and light. We teach them to be idealistic. Along come the cults and take these very qualities and exploit them to their profit. They have an enormous advantage simply because they lack integrity and principle.

A friend of mine recently picked up a newspaper at Western University. It is called *The Christian*. "He Brought Life To Me," is the title of an article on the front page; and "Safety, Certainty and Enjoyment" is on the second page. Other articles are called "Obedience to the Inner Voice," "How to Abide in Christ" and "The Church is One." The newspaper invites Christians to meetings each week. There isn't anything about the newspaper to suggest that "Christians on Campus" is anything but a group of young people gathered together for Christian fellowship. But when my friend looked into it, he discovered that this newspaper is in fact published by a very dangerous cult called "The Local Church." It started in China. It went to Formosa. It entered the United States at San Francisco and moved to Canada. Now, I am not disputing its right to exist. I am saying only that its approach is deceitful. Its leaders do not tell us who and what they are. So young people are deceived and drawn into a cult without knowing what it is they are getting into. Knowing that those who are deceitful have an advantage, Christians need to be more vigilant. We should remember that our Lord exhorted us to be "street smart," to be as harmless as doves and as wise as serpents.

At the same time, one can't help wondering why, if God really wanted to order the world properly, goodness should have such a steep uphill struggle all the time. Why do the unscrupulous, the liars and the cheats, seem to get the breaks? Why are the Christians in the arena and the dictators in the box seats? Why is truth so often on the scaffold and wrong forever on the throne?

These are the psalmist's complaints, but they are our complaints too. The psalmist cries out that if God really loved us, it wouldn't be like that. He is disappointed in God. So are many thoughtful people today. We may be disappointed in Him ourselves. Faith in God is not easy. We complain, as did Job and as did the psalmist, "Evil has come, though I expected good."

What do we say about this? Well, I begin by turning the psalmist's complaint on its head. The psalmist says that God doesn't love us enough to give us the kind of world we want. I say that God loves us too much to give us the kind of world we want. The psalmist says that if God's love were greater, He would make the righteous His favourites. He says that if God loved us more He would ensure that justice is done. I say that because God's love is so great He allows us to live in a world which often seems indifferent to good and evil. In other words, I claim that the very objections the psalmist makes to God's goodness are, in fact, expressions of His goodness.

The psalmist complains, for example, that God doesn't have favourites when He ought to. He ought to love the good people more and treat them better than the bad. Instead, He is indifferent; He makes His rain to fall on the just and the unjust and His sun to rise on good and bad alike. I say that this is so, not because He is indifferent, but because He loves everyone! Do we really want a God who plays favourites? Do we want a God who loves us more than He loves someone else, or who loves someone else more than He loves us? Would that increase or diminish God's love and your respect for Him? God doesn't have favourites for the simple reason that He loves every one of us with all the love He has. That's better, is it not? If He treats us impartially it is because each of us is as precious to Him as every other. Is that something to object to or to rejoice in? We admire such undiscriminating love when we see it in others. For example, suppose your daughter, a friend of my daughter, came to spend a few days in my home. Now there is no doubt that I love my daughter more than I love yours. But what would you think of me if I were to treat your daughter unfairly while she stayed with us? Suppose I made it painfully clear that my daughter was my favourite, and lavished upon her special favours which I withheld from your little girl? You wouldn't like that. I wouldn't like it either. It would be unkind and ungracious. We know that even if I love my daughter more than I love yours, nevertheless I must treat both of them lovingly, with fairness and thoughtful consideration, and if anything take special care to make our guest feel at home with us.

So it is with God. He doesn't love one of us more than the other. He doesn't even love us equally. He loves us uniquely. How then can we expect Him to play favourites? If He did, we should feel the wrongness of it. God ought not to do that. We must see His impartiality as the expression of His love, not of His indifference. And who would want to use religion to get special favours anyway? There is something ignoble about that, something small and despicable. William James spoke of those who "lobby for special favours in the courts of the Almighty." He thought it contemptible, and so do I. We ought not to use God to win an advantage over other people. We ought not to presume on the Almighty just because we have faith. It should offend us to think that God loves some more than others when every page of the New Testament declares that He loves each of His children with all the love He has. How can God have favourites when His favour rests on each of us?

Here is the second thing to notice about the psalmist's complaint. He contends that the world would be more moral if the righteous were rewarded with prosperity and the wicked punished. But I say that in such a world goodness would be unrecognizable, and disinterested goodness impossible.

Let us recall for a moment the woman who left the Christian church because the good man died young and the bitter old woman seemed to live forever. She thought that was a poor way for God to order things. But suppose life worked according to her prescription. Suppose you knew that if you were good you would live to a ripe old age and have good health and prosperity and security. Suppose you knew that if you were wicked, you would die young. Don't you think that would make goodness impossible? We should be unable to distinguish between goodness and self-interest. In those circumstances you would be stupid not to be good. This is what Sir Thomas More, the "Man for All Seasons," said to his daughter Meg. Like the psalmist, she had complained that good people, like her father, were afflicted and oppressed when they deserved to be honoured. Her father replied, "If we lived in a State where virtue was profitable, common sense would make us good, and greed would make us saintly . . . But since in fact we see that avarice, anger, envy, pride, sloth, lust and stupidity commonly profit far beyond humility, chastity, fortitude, justice and thought, and have to choose, to be human at all . . . why then perhaps we *must* stand fast a little . . ."

That brings me to my third disagreement with what the psalmist said. He declares that God should treat us justly by giving us what we deserve, and he complains that God is unjust because He doesn't do so. He says, "Let us have justice! Reward the righteous and punish the wicked!" But I say that it is in the greatness of His love that He doesn't treat us justly. I don't want Him to treat me justly because I can't live by justice. Nor can you!

You must have heard the story of the woman who went to have her picture taken and said to the photographer, "Try to do me justice." And the photographer, who was neither gallant nor discreet, said "Madam, what you need is not justice, but mercy." So do we all! We can't live by justice. I don't want justice because justice doesn't meet my need. I need mercy. If we require only justice, what happens to forgiveness? What happens to kindness? What happens to grace? These are the things by which we live. Without them, our friendships could not be sustained, our marriages would be in ruins, and every relationship in life would be soured. Do you really want what you deserve? Thank God my friends don't give me what I deserve. They treat me lovingly and mercifully and with understanding and forgiveness. The just man is too hard. That is why we love justice and hate the just man. Ian

McLaren speaks of one such who was "As upright as a marble pillar — and as cold and as hard." John Wesley once met a man who said to him, "I never forgive!" And Wesley's answer was delivered like a rapier-thrust, "Then you had better never sin!" It is Reinhold Niebuhr who reminds us that "Forgiving love is a possibility only for those who know they are not good, who feel themselves in need of divine mercy." Dostoevsky has one character say to another, "You have no tenderness, only justice, and therefore you are unjust." To to be truly just, justice must transcend itself and become kindness, mercy, love and forgiveness. There is an old legend that once God prayed; His prayer was, "May my justice be ruled by my mercy." Do you not see that if God treated us justly, if He gave us what we deserve, none of us could bear it? We live not by justice, but by grace.

And notice too the pretension in our demand for justice. We assume that we are the just. We are arrogant enough to separate the good and the bad, and to assume that we are among the good. We are like the conceited pharisee in our Lord's parable who paraded his virtue; he was so full of himself that he strutted in the Divine presence and thanked God that he was not as other men are. He was so good that all he needed was justice. But Jesus said that the pharisee's prayer went unheard. It never got off the ground. Let me tell you there is little warrant in our Lord's teaching for any easy assumption that we are among the good. How clearly He pointed this out in one of His greatest parables, that of the Last Judgement, when He said that the one thing we can be sure of is that there will be many surprises! We might take to heart the words of Reinhold Niebuhr who said that in God's eyes the difference between a good man and a bad man is insignificant. And this is true, not because sin is unimportant, but because all have sinned and all must live by the Divine mercy.

So there it is! Here is the psalmist saying that if God loved us He would order the world differently. I say to the psalmist that it is because God loves us so much that He orders it the way He does. I say it, because our Lord said it. He said it not only by His words but by His life. He showed us how a good man deals with an ambiguous world, a world where right and wrong do not always receive immediate reward and punishment.

Do you know what He did? He did four things. First, His expectations were realistic. He didn't expect special privileges. He expected a Cross and that is what He got. Not special favours or God looking after Him. That was, if you remember, one of the ways the devil tempted Him in the wilderness. He urged Him to throw Himself down from the pinnacle of the Temple so that God would intervene to save Him. This was a temptation which Jesus resisted. The life of our Lord was marked, not by special deliverance but by unusual suffering. And that is precisely what He promised His disciples. Our Lord did not hold out to them material rewards or physical security; He told them that those who followed Him must take up their cross and have a share in His suffering, His rejection and His death. St. Teresa expresses the truth of this with great power in *The Way of Perfection* when she says, "Fly a thousand leagues away from saying, ' . . . it was not *right* for me to suffer this, they had no *right* to do such a thing to me.' Now God deliver us from such wrong rights! Do you think that there was any question of rights when Jesus suffered the injuries which were so unrighteously inflicted on Him? . . ."

The second thing that Jesus did was to do good. He went about doing good. He didn't curse the darkness, He shone in it. He didn't complain about injustice, He took the things that were wrong and put them right. One day the people brought to Him a man who was blind and asked Him whose fault it was, his own or his parents. Our Lord spent no time at all trying to fix the blame or arguing the fairness or unfairness of the man's blindness; He simply reached out and healed him. He gave the man something better than an explanation; He gave him his sight!

That is our calling. The ills of life are an invitation to curse God and dispute His ordering of things, or they are an opportunity to become the instruments of His purpose by declaring His goodness and by putting things right. Which choice we make is our responsibility. There is no doubt what our Lord did with the evils of the world. He overcame them with good. If we call ourselves by His name, that is our work too.

Nor did Jesus treat people like children needing immediate rewards and punishments to sustain their faith. He knew that God had a nobler purpose for them. God had little interest in their security, comfort, or even peace of mind. But He was deeply interested in their integrity, fortitude and faithfulness. And so it is with us. He is much more interested in our character than in our comfort. Sometimes He denies us peace that He may give us glory!

Here is the last thing that Jesus did. He kept on trusting God. Even when it seemed that God had deserted Him, He didn't surrender His faith in His Father's goodness. Even when it seemed to everyone, Himself included, that God had disowned Him, He kept on believing in His love and mercy. And from the lips of our Lord in the place of His crucifixion there reaches us the prayer which every Jewish child prays in the evening, a simple prayer of confidence and trust: "Father, into thy hands I commend my spirit." Jesus offered up that prayer believing that it wasn't really the end, that God had something yet to do, and that He could be trusted, even at that terrible moment on Calvary, to do it.

And He did. A crucifixion became the world's salvation; a hill of torture shaped like a skull became a garden of resurrection. Transforming qualities of faith and love and hope are not easy. But you see, He not only asks them of us, but gives them to us and shares with us His victory.

THE EMPTY THRONE

"So you are a king?" said Pilate. "You!" "Certainly," said Jesus, "I am a king."

St. John 18:37 (Moffatt)

Today is Palm Sunday. The theme of Palm Sunday is Kingship. The first Palm Sunday was the day on which our Lord rode into Jerusalem and declared Himself King. But notice this: It was a rejected Kingship. A short time after He entered the city of Jerusalem to the sound of Hallelujahs and Hosannas, He wept. Wept over the same city. Why? Because Jerusalem had been false to its own name. The word Jerusalem means "Vision of Peace." But Jerusalem had lost her vision of peace. So the King who came riding in was not a crowned King but a rejected King. A weeping King. This brings me to the point I want to make on this Palm Sunday. Will you notice that even though Christ was a rejected King, the throne was not empty for long. Those who refused to crown Him were soon to cry, "We have no king but Caesar." If not Christ, then another would occupy the throne and reign from it.

This is the story of faith and this is the story of life. The throne is never empty for long. When we reject Christ, we quickly find somebody or something else to put in His place. Always there are those who would be king. Usurpers and pretenders.

This point is admirably captured in one of our Lord's parables. You remember how He told a story of a man whose house of life was inhabited, it was possessed by an evil spirit. Finally the man got fed up with it. He flung the demon out and he cleaned house, but he didn't do anything else. His house of life was empty. Swept, clean, and vacant. So the demon went away and quickly found seven spirits more evil than himself and said, "Look, here is a house left empty; let's take it over!" They took possession. And now the man had not one demon to contend with, but eight! Christ's verdict in that parable was, "The last state of that man became worse than the first."

We are all like that man. We think we can get rid of the yoke of religion; we think we can get rid of God, that we can do without a king. But suddenly we discover that it is not so easy. You see, it is not a choice between this king and no king; the real choice is what kind of king we shall serve. The truth of the parable applies not just to demons but to gods. We get rid of God, we say He is dead, we fling him from the house of our life. But we soon discover that if God is dead, the gods are not. So our empty house is filled up with all kinds of pale ghosts who take possession not only to rule, but to distort our lives. If we usurp the one true God, the King worthy of allegiance, we shall not remain without gods or without allegiances. We shall simply have inferior gods and base allegiances. That is my message this morning. I want to consider how it is that when people think they have got rid of God and say, "We shall have no king to rule us," they very soon discover that they cannot live without a sense of the transcendent, without symbols of the divine, without a realization that we are made for higher things. And so they elevate other values, symbols, ends, to occupy the place once filled by God.

Let me explain what I mean. Consider, first, how this works in religion. There are many who get rid of religion. They push it out of their lives and rejoice that they are free of its language, its practice, its superstition, its inhibitions. But soon they discover they cannot get on without it. Without some sense of the transcendent, they are consumed by their own insignificance. So what do they do? They discover another religion. Sometimes the other religion they discover is old. Did you know that there are two thousand – I am not making this up – two thousand witches in the city of Toronto? I read that in the *Globe and Mail*. In March 1984 the newspaper devoted a full page to witches in Toronto. A reporter went around and attended a coven of fifty-four witches. He watched them at their ceremonies. He discovered that some of these people were former members of the United Church and the Roman Catholic Church and the Anglican Church. But they had grown dissatisfied with the church and with religion. They decided to give it up. And now they had found the ancient gods and goddesses of Greece and Rome. So there they were, meeting together, witches in Toronto, Ontario, in 1984, chanting their incantations and casting their spells. They got rid of one religion alright, but quickly enthroned the oldest anti-religion in its place!

Now other people cast off the old religions and put new ones in their place. It has been pointed out to the point of weariness that many contemporary "isms" – fascism and communism, for example – are what Karl Barth once called "disguised religions." Sometimes they look like politics; often like the politics of power. But when we analyze them we discover, as Paul Scherer pointed out, that every Christian doctrine has its secular or ideological counterpart. They have heroes; they have saints and martyrs; they have rituals and high days. It is all there.

In a book about power, called *The Poisoned Crown*, the title taken from those marvellous lines of William Blake, "The strongest poison ever known/Comes from Caesar's laurel crown," Hugh Kingsmill grouped together the power maniacs of our time. Napoleon, Cromwell, Hitler, Nietzche, and old D. H. Lawrence, the pied-piper of sex, which, in a materialistic society, is the mysticism of the masses. Here they are, the pursuers of power who attempt to persuade us that power or sex or victory can be a vocation. It is the path to the future. It is the destiny of supermen. And then along comes a dying man on the Hebridean Island of Jura, George Orwell, who anatomizes just what sort of a vocation and what sort of a society would be the result and shows us Big Brother's Oceania full of men "who think in slogans and speak in bullets."

I hope my point is clear. We think we get rid of religion when in fact we substitute another religion, only worse. We remove one God who elevates us, who reminds us of our divinity, and, in Pascal's phrase, we "lick the earth" and put in His place demons or madmen or ideologues.

And then, of course, there is *the* secular religion of our time. It is another "ism." Humanism. By that I do not mean a belief which celebrates the richness of human achievement in music and art and literature. Such accomplishments are the good gift of God so that, in a sense, every Christian is a humanist. He believes that the glory of God is man fully alive. What I mean is the humanism that says we must shape our values and chart our destiny and make all our own decisions without reference to anything higher than ourselves. That is the humanism I despise, for it is a worship of the self.

This sort of humanism permeates our way of looking at life so much that often we don't even notice. For example, in the debate over whether religion will be taught in the schools. The truth is that we already teach religion in our schools, and the religion we teach is the religion of secular humanism. Now the point to notice here is that if this is so, then the ground of our discussion has changed. When we recognize that secular humanism is itself a religion, then the debate does not set faith against non-faith. It no longer sets the religious man over against the irreligious man. The question now is: *Which* religion? It is not religion or no religion. It is not this king or no king. Not this God or no God. Rather, it is which God will you worship? Which king will you serve? Which religion has your allegiance?

The second thing to notice is that this is also true of faith. Now, critics of Christianity are forever saying that faith is credulity. Faith is really for people who cannot, or will not, think for themselves. Like the proverbial school boy who said, "Faith is just believing what you know ain't true."

But if faith is just credulity, it would follow, would it not, that the most credulous people would be the most religious people. Yet the evidence is all against that. I think of St. Augustine and Soren Kierkegaard and William Blake and Blaise Pascal and Jonathan Swift — whatever adjective one might apply to such men, credulous will not do. And such examples could be multiplied a hundred-fold. One could almost say that the most profound Christians have been the most skeptical. I think of men like C.E.M. Joad, and C. S. Lewis and Malcolm Muggeridge, who did not welcome faith but were carried struggling and kicking into the Kingdom, casting about every moment for a way out.

Let me tell you that the best doubters I have known have not been outside the faith, but inside it. The most strenuous and rigorous objections to Christianity which I have heard have come not from atheists but from Christians. The deepest objections that have assailed me did not come from Bertrand Russell or from Madalyn Murray, but from my own heart and mind. Say, if you must, that faith is credulity, but you cannot make it stick.

I love what Malcolm Muggeridge said about his life-long friend Alec Vidler, a distinguished Anglican theologian. He said, "Alec is the quintessential Anglican. He believes with all his heart and doubts with all his mind." Faith may be compatible with credulity but, in my experience, and in the best believers, they are seldom found together.

Then we examine the substitutes for the Christian faith, the new religions and the isms. And what do we find? What is the nature and the stringency of their faith? The reporter who visited the witches in Toronto (is it not marvellous to be talking about witches in Toronto in 1984 — it pleases the medieval part of me!) read the advertisements on their notice board. They advertised a clairvoyant, and an astrologer, and a spiritualist, and a palmist. Skeptics all, I am confident. Listen to this one! They promoted an aroma therapist! I wonder what he does? They had an expert on Chinese numerology; another on life-cycle charts. They had a reader of tarot cards. These are the very people who charge Christians with credulity! I love the flashing sentence from Dr. John Short of Toronto who said once, "I am not credulous enough to be an atheist." G. K. Chesterton said the same thing in his own inimitable way by telling us that when people cease to believe in God, it is commonly supposed that they believe in nothing; alas, the truth is far worse: They believe in anything. No wonder Malcolm Muggeridge declares that the eighth deadly sin of our time is credulity!

Let me make this point more contemporary. Let's talk about Solzhenitsyn. He says that there is nothing more universally discredited today than Communism. Communism has been proved wrong in its predictions. It has been inept in its analysis, both of human nature and of society. It is utterly discredited in the Soviet Union today. No intellectual in Russia can seriously regard it as an ideology. So where do we find it? We find it in the West! We find it among so-called intellectuals in Western universities. The question is: How on earth can they believe it? And Solzhenitsyn tells us why. Because they crave faith. They long to belong to something bigger than themselves. So they affirm a discredited, empty ideology. And they illustrate my point that when you get rid of Christian Faith you are not done with faith. What happens is that you acquire another faith. It is not that when you are rid of God, your work is ended. Now you have to contend with the gods! Aristophanes knew it — when Zeus is dead, Whirl is King! There is a marvellous text on this very point in the Book of Judges. It says, "In those days, there was no king in Israel and every man did what was right in his own eyes." Is that not our predicament?

Let me tell you something else about faith. There is a meaning of faith that does not imply credulity but which recognizes faith as the very condition of knowledge. Faith, then, is not set over against reason but is the faculty by which reason does her work and without which knowledge is unattainable even by reason! Do you want an illustration of that? I can give you one by asking how much you can know of me without trusting me. You see, if all I meet in you is suspicion or hostility, then there will inevitably be things you are never going to know about me, because you are incapable of discovering them and I am unable or unwilling to reveal them to you. Your distrust makes intimate personal knowledge of me impossible. Only faith can make a relationship possible. If you haven't got it, you have no deep human relationships. So that if your basic attitude towards life and other people is one of inordinate suspicion, then you must not expect love or even friendship. Because all relationships are impossible without faith, openness, and trust. That is true, not only of those of us who claim to have religious faith; it is true of everyone. No one can have a human relationship or a loving existence without faith. Robert Frost wrote of his relationship with his wife that the two of them "believed it into fulfillment." Isn't that wonderful? Think of believing a relationship into fulfillment! All genuine relationships are like that. They are believed into fulfillment because faith is prior, it originates, it is the condition of knowledge, it makes everything possible.

Again, will you notice how, if this is true, the nature of our discussion has changed. We no longer have the man of faith confronting the person who has no faith; rather we all have some faith or we belie our humanity. So the question is no longer whether or not to have faith. We all do and we all must. Now the question is: Faith in what? Where do you put your faith? It is not that you have no king, but what king do you have? It is not that you have no God, but what kind of God do you trust? It is not that you have no faith, but whether or not the object of your faith is worthy of it.

This brings me to a third thing. What I have said is true not only of religion, not only of faith, but also of belief. Let me illustrate this by an incident from the life of the great theologian, Karl Barth. Barth and a distinguished atheist were asked to debate about belief. Do you know how Barth began? He did not begin by saying, "Right, you are an atheist, an unbeliever, and I am a Christian, a believer, and here is where we differ." No, he did something much more useful and clever. He said, "Let me for a moment tell you what you believe in." In other words, Barth's premise was that the atheist too was a believer, and that the real difference between them was in the quality of their beliefs. He then went on to reveal to this man that what he had elevated to the status of divinity was a belief in the rationality of man. He had elevated reason and he had infused this belief with all the meaning of God. Now, said Barth, you believe and I believe; the issue is what do we believe in!

I want to say the same thing to you. Some of you may call yourselves unbelievers; look, you have a god you believe in! There is something in your life to which you give your primary allegiance. There is something or someone you have raised to the level of divinity. You have what Paul Tillich called an "ultimate concern." Something makes your wheels go round. What is it that you are really after? Sometimes it is sex, sometimes it is power, sometimes it is fame, sometimes it is fashion, sometimes it is money, sometimes it is security. Whatever it is, there is something or someone to whom you have given your ultimate allegiance. Make no mistake about it, that is your god.

The question is, "Is he worthy of your allegiance?" Don't spend your life pursuing something too small because in the end it will leave you empty. Once again, the nature of the discussion has changed and will no longer allow us to set the unbeliever over against the believer. We are all believers. But what do you believe in? That's the question! And is what you believe in worthy of the divine spark in you or is it too small for your greatness?

That brings me to the last thing. What I have been saying is true, not only of religion and faith and belief, it is also true of worship. Very often people say, "Christians worship, but I don't. Christians are the people who go to church and sing the hymns and say the prayers and read the Scriptures. I don't do that. I am not a worshipper."

It simply is not true. Do you know why? Because to worship simply means to ascribe worth. That is what the word means. And everyone ascribes worth to something. Everyone!

It's a bit like reading and underlining a book. In a book you underline the bits you think are most important. Well, you do the same thing with your life. Every single life underlines something stands for something, affirms certain values. The question is not whether or not to worship; the truth is, everybody worships. The question is: What do you worship? Is it worthy of you? Does it really deserve the worth that you ascribe to it? A sad thing in a preacher's life is to encounter so many midget tragedies, people living for the wrong things who at last get everything they want and find they are still unsatisfied. You ought to know what your values are, what you are really after, because you just might get them! Will they be enough for you? Is what you are after great enough to sustain and satisfy a genuinely human existence, or are you "spending your money for that which is not bread and your labour for that which satisfieth not?" If the function of education is to teach us to appreciate what *ought* to be appreciated, then the meaning of Christian worship is to teach us to worship what *ought* to be worshipped. Keep this in mind, then, as you choose the values and ideals to which you will ascribe worth! Remember that selfishness will make your world very narrow indeed; that material values can yield no immaterial reward; that ends too small, and relentlessly pursued,will present you with a success that is also your punishment; that small gods can be worshipped only by small people; that you assume the character of the values you worship, and that anything you can really succeed at is too trivial to satisfy you.

There are other aspects of Christian worship which are common to both believers and unbelievers. Thanksgiving is one of them. It was G. K. Chesterton who said that one of the most terrible things about being an atheist is that you have no one to thank. But atheists are thankful anyway. I once heard a militant atheist thank God she was an atheist! Katherine Mansfield, who had turned from Christian belief and worship, once found herself in an Alpine meadow so beautiful that she longed to make "some small grasshoppery sound of praise to Someone or to Something." And Leslie Stephen, when his wife died and he remembered what a privilege it had been to know and love her, wrote, "I thank . . ." and then remembered that having surrendered faith there was no one to thank, but went on, "I thank *Something* that I loved her as heartily as I knew how to love." See how the heart goes out to the throne even as we affirm that the throne is empty!

The same thing is true of prayer. Unbelievers tell us that only believers pray, but that is nonsense. Unbelievers pray, too. And sometimes eloquently. Again, Chesterton complained that one of the drawbacks of being an atheist is that you cannot swear, for you have nothing to swear by. The best, or worst, you can manage is, "Oh, bother!" or something of the sort. And that isn't serious enough either for the depth of our sorrow or the height of our ecstasy. There are occasions when the only thing that will do is "Oh God!" And that's prayer! I am reminded of the splendid words of Job, "Does not one stretch out his hand in his fall?" And if you do, you're praying, believer or not!

C. S. Lewis once talked to his Rector about prayer. The Rector said that most people in his parish said only the same little childish prayers they had first learned at their mother's knee. Lewis was surprised. Surely that did not mean they hadn't something for which they were thankful, or for which they were truly penitent, or some great aching need? Yes, replied the Rector, they have all these, but such deep matters never reach the level of their prayers. So Lewis came to a somewhat startling conclusion. He concluded that the prayers we say may be the most irreligious part of us. Perhaps the truly religious part of us is the bit that groans and sighs and aches and yearns with things too deep for utterance. Perhaps those are the prayers God hears. The Apostle Paul tells us that God knows us at the level of our groaning.

Everyone prays. Everyone has yearnings that well up involuntarily. We all send shafts of pleading from the depths of our being without even knowing it. Don't tell me you don't pray. You pray. It's just that you don't know that you do.

I know a family in my congregation with three children, two girls and a boy. The boy went off to summer camp for the first time, and a week later the rest of the family drove down to visit him. They had a great visit, but the awful moment came to say goodbye. The wee fellow was homesick. The sisters missed their brother. As they drove away in the car one of the girls said through her tears, "I know what to do. Let's pray for him!" And the other little girl replied, "I *can't* pray for him. I'm too busy crying!" Oh, she prayed for him! Every tear was a prayer. We think we don't pray. The truth is we pray all the time at levels so deep we don't even know it.

A choice! Palm Sunday always presents a choice. Jesus or Caesar? Which king? Which faith? What to worship? Whom to thank? By whom to swear? The meaning of Palm Sunday — what infuses it with such joy — is that our presence here in this place answers these questions. By coming here we affirm that Jesus is King. Hosannah! Hosannah in the highest! Blessed is He who comes as King in the name of the Lord! He is our King and the throne is not empty!

WHO GOES THERE?

So we do not lose heart. Though our outer nature is wasting away, our inner nature is being renewed every day. For this slight momentary affliction is preparing for us an eternal weight of glory beyond all comparison, because we look not to the things that are seen but to the things that are unseen; for the things that are seen are transient, but the things that are unseen are eternal.

2 Corinthians 4:16–18

"Who goes there?" is the call of the sentry. So, too, is "Friend or foe?" Suppose we called out "Who goes there?" and received the answer, "Death!" Would that be the answer of a friend or a foe?

There is no doubt about what the Greek Philosophers would answer. Plato, for example, would say that death is a friend. Death is the great emancipator. Death comes to release the soul from the prison-house of the body, setting it free to go to the Eternal and Spiritual world which is its true home.

Who goes there? Death! Ah, friend!

There are many people in our time who think the same way. H. L. Mencken, for example, did not believe in immortality and had no desire for it. In a letter to Will Durant he asserted that the Christian belief in immortality issues from the puerile egos of inferior men. Similarly, Huxley mocked Christians by saying, "There are people who long for immortality and yet don't know what to do with themselves on a wet Sunday afternoon." Fred Hoyle, the distinguished physicist and astronomer used to say, "I have no desire for eternal life. If I had a choice, I think I would choose to live for more than seventy years. Perhaps I would choose to live for about three hundred. But not any more than that." Ralph Barton was an American cartoonist who committed suicide, and in the letter which he left to tell why he had done it he explained, "I have done this because I am fed up with inventing devices for getting through twenty-four hours every day."

So there is one answer which begins with Plato and reaches to the present time. "Who goes there, friend or foe?" Death! A friend.

But that is not the answer that most people would give today. To most people, death is an enemy. Malcolm Muggeridge says that death has become for us the dirty little secret that sex was to the Victorians. Death is the obscenity of our time. It is the thing we refuse to mention. Freud said that we just keep putting off the very thought of it until death is so near to us we haven't any choice. We "do not go gentle into that good night; we rage, rage against the dying of the light."

Or we say, "Everybody dies, but we live on in the memory of other people." Of course we do, for a short while. But not in many memories, and not for long. The other day I counted up those who remember my grandfather. I think there are six people left who knew him, and they are all old, and before long they will die and he will be forgotten.

Or we say that we live on in our influence on other people; rather like good teachers who deeply influence their students. I was astonished just last week to notice this view advanced by a Christian preacher as a belief in immortality. It is no kind of immortality at all because the truth is that we live on through our influence for only a very short time. Notice also that our living on in the lives of other people presupposes that there will always be people alive who were influenced by us, directly or indirectly. But we know that this is not something we can take for granted. Even if we manage to get through the next few years without blowing up the world, the astronomers tell us that sooner or later we shall all die. We are not sure whether it will be by fire or ice, but one way or another there will be an end to the human race, and whatever diluted influence we had will be lost forever. What a pale substitute for immortality it is to say that our influence continues when we ourselves are dead!

These are some of the ways we attempt to reconcile ourselves to death. None of them work. They don't work because they are superficial and untrue. We sense their emptiness even as we state them. And all the time there is a much better way of facing death. Malcolm Muggeridge and his friend Alec Vidler were once walking in Ireland when they came upon an old Irish woman sitting outside her thatched cottage. She was well on in years, and Muggeridge asked her what she was doing. Without any hesitation she said, "I am learning how to die!" Her answer made a profound impression on Muggeridge; so much so that he, who is the least morbid of men, would say that in all his living, he is learning how to make a good death.

Emily Dickinson, in one of her poems, talks about "the overtakelessness of those who have *accomplished* death." Death isn't something you try to avoid, and it isn't merely something that happens to you. It is something you accomplish. Dag Hammarskjold speaks of living in such a way as to make death a *fulfillment*. It is impossible to evade the reality of death, because as every philosopher has told us clearly, the way we think about death determines how we think about life. How we think about the end of everything shapes our values and sets our priorities. So what are we going to do about death? How are we to think of it? Is it friend or foe?

Let there be no mistake, Easter has to do with whether death is friend or enemy. We sometimes think that Easter is about Spring. To some extent that is true. "Lent," which leads up to Easter, means lengthening; it welcomes the stretching out of the days and the warmth of the returning sun. But Easter is about life and death. It answers our question "Friend or Foe?" by declaring that death is a defeated enemy. That is the heart of the Christian Gospel, and it makes all the difference not only to how we die, but to how we live.

This becomes apparent as soon as we examine the Easter vocabulary of our hymns and prayers and readings from the New Testament. Easter is a Victory, a Triumph. Christ is the Conqueror who has overcome death and brought life and immortality to light. The Easter message announces to us that death has been robbed of the power it once had over us, so that it is no longer the horror it used to be. "O death, Where is Thy sting? O grave, where is thy victory? . . . Thanks be to God, who giveth us the victory through our Lord Jesus Christ." We know that the Eternal loves us, and that He loves us eternally. That does not mean only that He has given us life that doesn't end. Eternal life is not to be measured merely by quantity and duration. Unending life could just as easily be hellish as heavenly! What's the point of having immortal life if it's like waiting forever in a railway station? Who would want it? Eternal life means that God gives us His own quality of life, and because it is His life in us it is stronger than death. That is the Easter message.

For this reason we say that death is neither friend nor foe. Death is a defeated enemy. But of course, once your enemy has been defeated, you can make him your friend. We know this from recent history. You remember when we fought the Germans and the Japanese in the Second World War the conflict was bitter and total because they were our enemies and threatened our life and freedom. But once they were defeated, once they could no longer menace us, all kinds of opportunities presented themselves to treat them as friends. We could trade with them. Some of us drive Japanese cars. And those of us who drive Japanese cars do so because we can't afford German ones. Not only so, but those who were once our enemies could come to this country and become citizens of Canada. Once our enemies were defeated, they became our friends. A woman once chastised Abraham Lincoln severely for his magnanimous treatment of the South after the Civil War. She said to him, angrily, "Your responsibility is not to be kind to your enemies, but to destroy them!" And Lincoln replied, "But Madam, do I not destroy my enemies when I make them my friends?"

Something like that is what we have done with death. Once our enemy, it has been defeated and may now be regarded as our friend. We need not be afraid of it, for it no longer has an ultimate power over us. Notice how the resurrection of Christ has conquered death and altered its significance forever.

Why was death our enemy? I am going to mention five reasons, and here is the first one. Death was our enemy because it was the limit of our life. Martin Heidegger, the German existentialist philosopher, called death "The iron ring around existence." It is the limit which defines all our possibilities. Everything that we hope to accomplish is bound by that horizon. There isn't anything beyond it.

Albert Camus would agree with Heidegger. He said, "We hate death because it makes the lie definitive." What lie? The lie that we have endless time in which to do all we want to do: improve our brains, reform our character, fulfill our ambitions, go everywhere, see everything, and meet everybody. Death mocks all those pretensions. We hate it because it gives the lie to the old Irish saying that when God made time He made plenty of it. Death reminds us that we run out of time before we have done all that we hoped to do.

This is sometimes brought home to us with enormous power. I once visited a young woman in hospital who had undergone certain tests and was awaiting their outcome. The result was a matter of life and death for her. If the tests were negative her life would go on as before. If they were positive she had only a very short time to live. She said to me, "The difficult thing is that this may be the end of my life and I haven't done all the things I had counted on doing. It isn't that I am afraid of death; it is just that my life feels so unfinished."

Sir John Barbirolli and André Previn were once flying in a jet airplane when it was caught in a violent thunderstorm. None of the passengers thought they would survive. Sir John was indignant. He declared that it was inconceivable that he should die on that particular evening because he hadn't finished his latest cycle of recordings! Suddenly there is a limit where we hadn't expected one, and we find it enormously disconcerting. If someone were to tell me that this is the last sermon I would ever preach, my reaction would not be one of fear but of incredulity. This *couldn't* be my last sermon for I have a head-full of ideas for half-a-dozen magnificent sermons which the world simply must hear! So it is with all of us. Death is the iron ring around existence. We have places to go, things to see, books to read, visions to realize, hopes to fulfill. And suddenly we are confronted with our own mortality and we are forced to face up to the fact that we have run out of time.

> To leave unseen so many a glorious sight,
> To leave so many lands unvisited,
> To leave so many worthiest books unread,
> Unrealized, so many visions bright —

Oh! wretched yet inevitable spite
Of our short span . . .

Easter proclaims that that threat of death has been removed, that the "iron ring around existence" has been snapped and no longer sets the limit of our possibilities. In his letter to the Philippians, Paul tells us that God, who has started a good work in us, will bring it to fulfillment. That is Christian Hope. God has taught us to love a little bit; He will allow no limit to close off our love, but will teach us to love more and more. He has gathered us into His friendship so that we know Him a little; He won't allow that friendship to end just because we die. We have started our education in this "vale of soul-making" and are growing wiser, deeper, stronger; God will not allow death to put a stop to that. We have known the creative impulse and have done something with it, but we know that even our best was little more than a hint, a promise, something started but pointing forward to something better. And God will not allow that flowering of our spirit to be smothered. Can you believe that because of Easter nothing good or precious in us will ever be lost? All the promise and unfulfilled expectancy of our lives will be gloriously consummated because death has been defeated.

Now once we believe that, death really can become our friend. For one thing, it sets a manageable limit to life when we understand that it is not the *ultimate* limit. Fred Hoyle asked for three hundred years of life instead of seventy. I should find three hundred years on earth too long. Would you want three centuries of life here? I wouldn't know how to cope with three hundred years. How could I gather into my life and experience all that has happened since 1685? But I can cope with seventy years very nicely. So many years for this and so many for that. It's a bit like having our friends come to visit. The first thing we need to know is how long they can stay. We need to know, because the length of their stay determines where we can go and what we can do. Once we have determined our limits we can choose our priorities and plan our activities.

Life itself is like that. We move forward to our horizon of threescore years and ten, and then back to where we are now, and determine what is possible between now and then. Samuel Johnson said, "The prospect of a hanging wonderfully concentrates a man's mind." Indeed it does! It forces us to decide what is of greatest importance. The other day I read an article by a woman who was told she had only a short time to live. She wrote a piece called "My Last Wonderful Days," in which she tells us what she would do if she could live over again. She would make more time for beauty; for flowers and sunsets. She said she would give up many of her outside activities to become the serene core of her home. And she would get to know people a lot faster than before, because people matter more than anything else, and time is short. So it is that death which once threatened us by appearing to be the limit beyond which we could not go becomes a friend, giving shape to our life and helping us to concentrate our mind and choose our priorities.

Well, that's one of the threats of death. Another one is that it takes our loved ones from us. This is the most terrible threat of all. H. L. Mencken was simply wrong when he said that our desire for immortal life is puerile egotism. Most of the time it isn't egotism at all, it's love. It is love that cries out for immortal life. It is that you love someone and because you love them you can't bear that you should lose them or that they should be lost. Tolstoy has Prince Andrey express this longing in *War and Peace.* The Prince says, "One is convinced of the necessity of a future life, not by argument but when one goes hand-in-hand with someone, and all at once that someone slips way yonder into nowhere, and you are left facing into the abyss and looking down into it."

That's what is so frightening about loving. How vulnerable we are when we love somebody! "He that hath wife and child hath given hostages to fortune," cried Francis Bacon, and we have all felt that, for we never know when death will come to snatch them away. And death still has that power. Death is a terrible reality. Christians are not interested in denying its reality, but in declaring the limits of its power. Christians believe that death does not have the power finally, ultimately, to separate us from those we love. We may be separated from them for a little while, but because God's love is stronger than death there is no final separation. That is the message of the New Testament. So it is that Christians, instead of being appalled and overwhelmed by this threat of death, simply transfer their affections from this life to the next, from earth to heaven. Their love follows their dear ones to the eternal world, and they wait in hope, knowing they shall be reunited with them on another shore.

When C. S. Lewis lost his dear friend Charles Williams, he wrote something which he said he thought he would never write, because before that he would have considered it sentimental claptrap. He wrote that since Charles Williams died, heaven was no longer a strange, far-off place. It had been that once, but now it was near and dear and familiar because his friend was there. When Lewis lost his wife Joy he said the same thing again. Heaven was closer still, for Joy was there. All Christians do this. We lose our brothers and sisters, our parents and friends. And one by one those whom we love move from this world to another world. More than half our life goes with them, so that our thoughts become centered not on earthly things, but on heavenly things and on all our friends who are in heaven and who wait for us there.

It was in 1958 in the little fishing village of Donaghadee on the County Down coast of Northern Ireland that I first met Mrs. Bunting. She was well over eighty years of age. I shall never forget how she said to me, "Mr. Boyd, I am not afraid to die because I have a claim in heaven." Do you know what her claim was? It was her own child who had died in infancy. Mrs. Bunting had lived to be a ripe old age but all the time she had loved that little one. She was not afraid to die because she had a claim in heaven; there was a little bit of herself already there.

The truth is that we all have a claim in heaven. All our dear ones, those we have "loved long since and lost awhile," are our claim. Sometimes people ask me, "When I die shall I know my dear ones and shall I be able to love them?" And I answer with another question, "Would it be heaven if you didn't and couldn't?" Of course we shall know them and love them! We shall know them even better there than we have known them here. We shall love them more. To be in heaven is to know our powers of loving increased, not diminished. A great Methodist preacher, Dr. W. E. Sangster of Westminster, once wrote a note to his wife at Easter. It said, "You know we don't give Easter presents because Easter itself is the best present. It tells us that we shall be able to love each other for ever and ever."

The title sermon in this book uses the words that Robert Frost chose for his tombstone, "I had a lover's quarrel with the world." Some time later a member of our church went and took a picture of the tombstone and gave it to me. Under the poet's epitaph has been added his wife's name, and under his wife's name her epitaph, "Together wing to wing and oar to oar." Those words are true of our close relationships, not only in time, but in eternity. Death has no power over them. Ultimately, it cannot separate us from those we love.

Here is the third threat of death. It kills our bodies. There is no doubt about that. Paul puts it quaintly by telling us that "our outward humanity is in decay." That's a bit strong, don't you think? But it is certainly true that we are getting older, and it shows. Now we have grey hair that used to be black, and we wear two pairs of spectacles and a hearing aid. Of course there are more and more ways of renewing our bodies or denying the fact that we are getting older. We have false teeth. Kidneys and hearts and hair are transplanted, and there are lotions, potions and vitamins of every shape, size and colour to fight the ravages of time. There are some people walking around today with hardly anything they started out with. Like vintage cars they are patched up with new parts, wheezing and coughing occasionally, but still mobile. But only for a while. We know that whatever we do, we grow old and our physical powers diminish. It is not easy to reconcile ourselves to this. Some of my friends could express their attitude to death very clearly in the words of Sir Thomas Browne who said, "I am not so much afraid of death as ashamed ot it." Isn't that well put? *Ashamed* of it! Because all their lives they prided themselves on their health and vitality, their sharpness and vigour. Now they observe their powers diminishing, they can no longer do the things they used to do. But their mental age has not caught up with their physical age, and they cannot accept the fact that they are as old as they are. So they are not so much afraid of death as ashamed of it. That is one of death's most frightening powers. It kills the body.

But again, the significance of that threat has been changed. You see, Paul tells us not only that "our outward humanity is in decay," but that "day by day we are inwardly renewed." In other words, there are more ways to measure your age than by the weakness of your body. What about the strength of your spirit and the vitality of your soul? What if you measure your years by increasing grace and wisdom so that, as Socrates said, "you have adorned your soul with temperance and justice and are already preparing it for a higher and better world?" Then, however ashamed you may be at the work of death in you, you will be strengthened and encouraged by the increase of life in you. It happens all the time. I see it frequently. I have watched many people die, and there have been some whose diminishing physical strength was accompanied by increasing spiritual vitality. As their bodies failed, as they became quite literally in the words of the old song "a dear ruin," their spirit burned more brightly, and there was a kind of luminosity about them that was marvellously impressive and appealing. They discovered and have taught me that if there is a glory of the morning, the evening, too, has a splendour of its own. It was Sir William Mulock, Chief Justice of Canada, who said on his ninetieth birthday, "I am still at work with my face to the future. The shadows of evening lengthen. . . but the morning is in my heart . . . The testimony I bear is this, the best of life is further on, hidden from our eyes beyond the hills of Time." With such a faith, death's threat to kill our bodies loses its power to frighten us. "O death, where is thy Sting? O grave where is thy victory?"

Here is the fourth threat of death! It constitutes a threat to the self. Not only to my body, but to me, to R. Maurice Boyd, to this real person, this character, this personality, this unique, unrepeatable self. You substitute your name for mine and that is the threat of death to you. It is that the self should perish, should be irretrievably lost. And that's a terrible menace.

But, again, this threat has been overcome. It has been overcome because if we have been delivered from our concern about this self, there is little left for death to threaten. There is nothing for it to get a hold on.

In Markings Dag Hammarskjold tells us that there was an occasion in his life when he said 'yes' to Someone or Something and at that moment gave himself away. His life discovered a meaning in self-surrender. From that day on there was nothing that could threaten or harm him. Even courage ceased to have any meaning, because nothing could be taken from him. Death was no threat because in a sense he had already died. There was nothing for death to latch on to; there was no threat that it could utter because there was nothing to threaten. So it was with Hammarskjold, and so it may be with us.

There was a time in your life when you yourself were the center of your concern, and the focus of your interest. Then you met someone and fell in love with them. Suddenly, of all faces there was only one face. Of all forms, there was only one form. Of all voices, only one voice. Of all presences, only one presence. And the center of your life was no longer yourself, but another. In a sense, you died to yourself and you came alive for them. Then when children were born you discovered very quickly that you loved them more than you loved yourself. You would count it life's highest privilege to die for them if you had to. You would rather be ill yourself than have them sick. Because your own life means less to you than they do. In one sense you have died already. You have died to yourself and you have come alive to those you love. That is what the French poet meant when he told us that whoever knows the meaning of love knows the meaning of death. To love is to die to yourself, it is to know your concern centered on someone else who is dearer to you than your own life.

It is a bit like that when you really listen with great care to what somebody else is saying to you; you die to yourself a little and come alive for them. You "lend your mind out," in Browning's lovely phrase, and for a little while are hardly aware of yourself. That quality of self-forgetfulness is a hint of what it means to die to oneself and come alive to others. When that happens, death has nothing left to attack. Says George MacDonald, "You will be dead so long as you refuse to die." What is that but an echo of our Lord's words who told us that we shall possess our life if we fling it away, and we shall truly have it only when we are prepared to lose it.

St. Paul said the same thing. For him, "to live is Christ, and to die is gain." Death had no longer any power over him. Indeed death could but send him to be with Christ, "which is far better."

That brings me to the last threat of death. It keeps on reminding us of our mortality, and by reminding us of that, it casts a long shadow over our life.

You remember that when Gulliver came to Lilliput he discovered the people there were constantly afraid, always anxious. Would the sun swell up and engulf their world? Would a passing comet strike the earth and destroy them? And so every day they would talk about the catastrophes that might happen and bring about their death. They couldn't get away from the sense of their own mortality, and it poisoned their life.

There are plenty of Lilliputians. Do you remember how Kierkegaard described for us how we go to parties and have a happy time? But sooner or later we come back to our own room and in that midnight hour when all masks come off we know that we are afraid, burdened with this sense of our own mortality. In the Broadway Musical, *A Little Night Music*, the grandmother proposes a toast. "To life!" she says, and everyone at the dinner-party enthusiastically joins her. Then she proposes a second toast, saying, "And now a toast to the only other reality, death!" There is silence. The others cannot join that toast. They are fearful and embarrassed. The party is over.

Once again, the gospel declares that this threat has been taken away. It has been taken away because in Christ we have a sense not only of our mortality but of our eternal life in Him.

Hugh Kingsmill was one of Malcolm Muggeridge's dearest friends. In the company of another friend, he travelled once to the north of England and into Scotland. As they sat together in the train they talked about immortal life, about resurrection, about heaven, and life beyond the grave. Kingsmill's friend went into convoluted and difficult arguments for and against immortality. Kingsmill listened and then said something very simple and powerful. He said, "There are times when I have felt in my bones my own mortality. I believe it. And then there are hours, fewer but nevertheless real, when I have felt in my bones my own immortality. If I believe the former, why should I doubt the latter?" Why indeed! For the resurrection of Jesus Christ tells us that this sense of eternal life in us is the truth of us. We have longings which nothing in this world can satisfy and we begin to suspect that this is so because we were made for another world. We have seen visions too beautiful to be untrue. All our life we have been surprised by joy and haunted by intimations of immortality. How is it that our dreams are so much better and finer and nobler than we are? They are the truth of us, as the poetry in us is the truth of us, deeper than the dull prose. Easter declares that we are not only children of time, but nurslings of immortality; not creatures of an hour but sons and daughters of the Eternal; created, not to wither into dust and nothingness, but to be transformed from glory into glory, until we bear the very likeness of God.

So let me tell you as honestly as I can that by believing these things with all my heart death has no terrors for me. I want to live. I hope to live for a long time. But I am not afraid to die. I believe that it will be a great adventure, and that there will be splendid company on the other side. Have you ever read the words of C. S. Lewis with which he closes his stories of Narnia? You parents will have read them to your children when they were small. Read them again, for your own sake. Do you remember how the children and their parents have been killed in an accident? Aslan the Lion speaks softly to tell them that they are dead; that the term is finished, the holidays have begun; that the dream is over and now it is morning. Lewis writes:

> And for us this is the end of all the stories, and we can most truly say that they all lived happily ever after. But for them it was only the beginning of the real story. All their life in this world and all their adventures in Narnia had only been the cover and the title page; now at last they were beginning Chapter One of the Great Story, which no one on earth has read; which goes on for ever; in which every chapter is better than the one before.